SOUTH SUDAN:

BEYOND ETHNIC AND POLITICAL INERTIA

PETER LAM BOTH

The publisher wishes to acknowledge and thank Dr Douglas H. Johnson for his invaluable help and support for Africa World Books and its mission of preserving and promoting African cultural and literary traditions and history. Dr Johnson and fellow historians have been instrumental in ensuring that African people remain connected to their past and their identity. Africa World Books is proud to carry on this mission.

ISBN: 978-0-6453988-0-9 (Paperback)
978-0-6454529-9-0 (Hardcover)

Cover design, typesetting and layout : Africa World Books

TABLE OF CONTENTS

RISING FROM
THE ASHES OF WAR

Review of Peter Lam Both's
South Sudan: Beyond Ethnic and Political Inertia

By Francis M. Deng

PETER LAM BOTH'S BOOK, *South Sudan: Beyond Ethnic and Political Inertia* is a 'must read' for anyone concerned with the violent conflict that erupted in South Sudan in December 2013, less than two years after its independence on July 9, 2011, and has devastated the country ever since. The conflict has largely been viewed as ethnic, pitting the Dinka under the leadership of President Salva Kiir Mayardit, and the Nuer, led by his First Vice President, Dr. Riek Machar. I find the book very impressive and compelling not because the subject it is addressing is new, but because of the insight, the details, the nuances, and the objectivity the author brings to the discussion of the issues involved. The book is well written with lucidity and clarity that makes it a very compelling reading.

I first got to know Peter Lam when the National Dialogue Leadership assigned me the responsibility of chairing an Ad-Hoc Committee whose objective was to bring on board all the political parties, both in the government and in the opposition, to join the National Dialogue. The opposition parties had understandably boycotted the National Dialogue which they saw as the initiative of the ruling party, specifically the President, to polish the image of the regime. After the Revitalized Peace Agreement that was signed in Addis Ababa on September 12, 2018, it was thought opportune to invite all the parties to join the National Dialogue. But political agendas and aspirations differed, and the National Dialogue remained controversial. The task to which I was assigned was therefore very challenging. Although Peter Lam represented the ruling Sudan People's Liberation Movement (SPLM), he was most effective in bridging the differences through a thoughtful, objective, and constructive analysis and presentation of the case for a unified approach. He was catalytic to the success of our Ad-Hoc Committee. Peter Lam's treatment of the conflict that has bedeviled the country reflects elements that had impressed me in the role he played in the Committee.

Lam addresses, head on, the issue of whether the conflict is driven by ethnic differences and competition or by the ambitions and rivalries of the politicians. He does so with meticulous analysis of the perspectives of the individual leaders involved, their ambitions and the legitimate concerns of their ethnic communities – neither of which should be taken lightly.

I have always been intrigued by the interplay between the role of political entrepreneurs and the legitimate grievances of the ethnic groups they purportedly represent in identity-related conflicts. Political scientists generally contend that ethnic conflicts are driven by politicians exploiting ethnicity and not by ethnicity itself. This is usually linked with the tendency to dismiss or downplay ethnic identity as a significant variable in conflict analysis and resolution, allegedly because the concept is viewed as too nebulous and intangible, difficult to define, and therefore not a meaningful subject of negotiation. This amounts to dismissing ethnicity, or the broader concept of identity, as a fictional construct that has no real existence.

It has always been my view that one cannot exploit what does not exist and that it is not only unrealistic, but indeed offensive and dangerous to deny the existence of ethnicity or other forms of identity. What seems to be overlooked or underestimated is the fact that the distribution of power and material assets is often based on identity, whether racial, ethnic, cultural, or religious or defined by any other factors. What is critical then is not the mere fact of identity differences, but how those differences are managed.

With respect to South Sudan, Peter Lam articulates the problem very succinctly when he writes:

> *It is tribalism that threatens national unity and stability, not the tribes per se. Tribalism therefore is a manipulative method used by political leaders to mobilize their ethnic groups against others in order to gain their political objectives in a given country.*

As he elaborates:

> *Though the main driver of the conflict was a power struggle between and among leaders within SPLM as to who should lead the country after the independence was achieved, certain leaders presented the problem to their people as an ethnic conflict.*

So, what precisely is it in tribal or ethnic identity that the politicians exploit? I believe it is the sense of collective grievance against inequality emanating from mismanagement of diversity. This is often reflected in allegations of intolerable injustice in the shaping and sharing of power, national wealth and other values, material or intangible, and even symbolic. Injustice means that some groups enjoy the full rights of belonging to the national identity framework, while others are discriminated, marginalized and even excluded from fully sharing the rights of citizenship. The alleged inequality may only be perceived rather than real, but that does not prevent the entrepreneurs from exploiting it with what Peter Lam describes as a 'myopic view' of the leaders, backed by ill-informed mass following.

In South Sudan, the author maintains that:

> *The war was fought predominantly along ethnic lines as though ethnicity were the cause. Due to this myopic view of the conflict, it was difficult for many South Sudanese leaders to remain objective and view the conflict for what it was. Instead, they presented it to their people as war between the Nuer and Dinka which was not true. As a consequence, many South Sudanese people lost their lives*

believing that they were fighting an ethnic war. They did not know that they were fighting for the interest of their leaders to gain power. The worst thing was that by the time some of them realized, it was too late. The genie had already left the bottle. The country had already caught up in flames.

Lam asserts that the politicians in fact knew that what they were saying to mobilize their people was not true. So, in fact, they were misleading them, which underscores the element of exploitation as Peter Lam narrated:

South Sudanese leaders who advocated and called this war ethnic knew that it was not true. They knew that such description was deceptive, yet they used it to discredit the South Sudanese body politic as a Dinka system in order to have the legitimacy to mobilize their ethnic bases for support to challenge the government militarily. As is well known, the Government of South Sudan has never been a Dinka government. It represents South Sudanese people across the world. This narrow characterization of war as being ethnic was influenced by opposition leaders, activist groups, authors of books and articles on the war in South Sudan, as well as reports by international human rights and humanitarian organizations which were influenced by the agenda of the opposition political parties.

What I find ironic is that Peter presents the situation in a balanced way that defies the usual characterization of the war as senseless, reckless or irrational, when in fact the principal actors have a clear opportunistic calculation of what they are doing, wrong or even immoral as it may be. If one recognizes the designs and strategies of the opposition in their ruthless drive to gain power, one must also appreciate the counter measures of the government and its leadership to defend and retain its power. The arguments often levied against the leadership therefore does not adequately consider survival defense mechanism against perceived existential threat posed by armed insurgencies. Peter Lam makes the reader appreciate the point of view of every actor, whether or not you sympathize with them or vehemently disagree with their position. But, of course, rights and wrong are never equal! Nor does Lam claim moral equivalence in the position of the adversaries. In fact, he and some Nuer colleagues took sides with the Dinka-led government and suffered the consequences.

Indeed, one of the most moving aspects of Lam's account is the predicament those who rise above factionalism to promote the cause of unity and the common good of the nation face in sharply divisive identity-related conflicts. As he put it:

> *Standing for the unity and interest of the country in an ethnically charged environment like South Sudan in 2013 was very challenging. On the one hand, logic and reason dictate that we are all South Sudanese, and our allegiance should be to all our people in the country regardless of their ethnicity. But, on the other hand, one also belongs to a particular ethnic group just like the other leaders who stand in support of their ethnic bases. The two loyalties should naturally complement each other as they are mutually reinforcing. But this has not been the case in South Sudan*

*where conflict proliferated along ethnic lines. Supporting
the interest of the country at the apparent expense of one's
ethnic interest was uncommon, and it made others to
question our mental equanimity.*

Peter Lam does not hide or dismiss his identity as a Nuer. Far
from it, he acknowledges it and upholds it as a basis for his responsibility to work for the interest of both sides of the conflict
whose members he sees as equal fellow citizens to whom he
owes equal responsibility of leadership:

*For us, logic and patriotism dictate that our people are the
people of South Sudan as a whole, not just the Nuer. We
were troubled by the way our people were killing themselves in the country in various locations. We knew that the
Nuer were killed and so were other South Sudanese in the
Nuer areas. Our concern was to end the war quickly before
it could destroy even more lives.*

Unfortunately, that patriotic leadership is often not appreciated by most people on both sides. It can indeed be a very
painful and lonely position which only exceptional courage
and determination can sustain. I witnessed this position with
one of Peter's Nuer Colleagues, General James Hoth Mai, who
was the Chief of General Staff during the war that was seen as
pitting his people against the Dinka. I was very impressed by
what he was doing and indeed I often voiced my praise for
him in circles that included Dinka. I was shocked to hear some
people express opposite views against him, even accusing him
of undermining the fighting capacity of the army. When I first

met him in his office, General James Hoth told me that even before the outbreak of the violence, he had been under pressure from the Nuer who wanted to go to war with the Dinka over their grievances and that he was being criticized for remaining on the wrong side of an ethnic war. As Peter explains:

> *Their patriotic standpoint was the exception not the norm. Their position became so unorthodox that its validity was questioned by many Nuer and leaders from other ethnic groups as being too utopian. For taking such a stand, they were disowned and isolated by both sides to the conflict. The Nuer community ...deleted their names from the community list as in their view, we became 'Dinkas' since we did not support their cause.*

Particularly painful was the way they were not only rejected by the Dinka, but also marginalized by the government in which they were serving. I quote Lam's words in detail because I believe his message must be impressed upon the conscience of every fellow citizen as an important experience from which to draw crucial lessons to guide future conduct. Thus:

> *It could have made sense if the government and a majority of our Dinka colleagues in power reciprocated our patriotic resolve and standpoint. However, we had less, if not, non-existent recognition and support from the Government of South Sudan and the SPLM at that time. Even an acknowledgement of our role as stated above by the government could have made the difference. Instead, the government isolated us with the exception of new found SPLM*

Nuer members who were originally from NCP (the ruling party in the Arab Islamic regime in the Sudan). Some elements in the government thought we did not leave the government because we were trapped. They assumed we were waiting for Dr. Riek Machar to take over power so that we could join him. They totally misunderstood our resolve and commitment to this country and the SPLM. We remained here for South Sudan and not for anything else.

Marginalized by their own government, and rejected by their Dinka compatriots, they were truly in an identity void:

For a majority of our Dinka brothers and sisters, we were 'Nuer' and nothing else. The fact that our presence legitimized the Government of South Sudan which they led couldn't come close to the mind of those running the government. Our state of affairs in government was in jeopardy confirming what my friend at the United Nations Office in South Sudan told me in December 2013 'that the political victims of this war would be the Nuer patriots because they belonged to nobody, but the country.'

And, of course, to the Nuer, they were nothing short of traitors for the ethnic cause of their people:

The Nuer in opposition fumed with anger towards us for not supporting the cause of Dr. Riek Machar or joining them in the war of revenge. In fact, they could not get their heads around the reason why we refused to join them. They said that we were bought by Dinka to stay aloof from the war. Hence, they coined the term 'Nuer wew' or as Pendle (2020) put it frankly, 'Nuer of Dinka Money' to describe us. For them, we became their enemy number one. In their social media writings and video postings where they incite the Nuer to revenge and kill the Dinka, they never missed the opportunity to take a swipe at us. 'We will get you. We will kill you first before the Dinkas.'

The case of South Sudan represents the dilemma of identity and diversity which is widely shared in varying degrees by many countries. I witnessed this in my two United Nations mandates, first as Representative of the Secretary General on Internally Displaced Persons for twelve years and then as Special Advisor of the Secretary General for the Prevention of Genocide. In my field missions around the world, I saw the crisis of national identity manifested in the conflict between aspirations for national unity and the demand for equality and even self-determination by minorities. I am often left wondering how those identity groups in conflict would ever get together to become one united nation.

The constructive way out of the conundrum of such conflicts is not to deny the existence of ethnicity or identity, but to ensure inclusivity, equality, and respect for the dignity of all groups, without discrimination on any ground. This was in essence the New Sudan ideal the people of the Sudan, led by South Sudanese, were fighting for. The vision of a 'New' dispensation of full equality is one which virtually every country in the world, not least South Sudan, desperately needs. It is by invoking gross inequality that political entrepreneurs exploit ethnicity or identity for their self-interested ambitions for power and wealth. But since perceptions do not necessarily reflect facts, remedial measures must be accompanied by mass education and political enlightenment on the facts to guard against false allegations by politicians.

In addressing the perceived grievances, we must look for guidance to our fundamental cultural values and normative principles of conflict management and resolution. Our cultures of South Sudan have been thoroughly studied by anthropologists, although we have unfortunately not made effective use of those studies. Peter Lam in fact refers to some of the major concepts that have been documented in the anthropological studies of our societies. Among these are such notions as acephalous political systems, stateless societies, tribes without rulers, the segmentary lineage system, balanced opposition, and ordered anarchy. These concepts, which our people have sometimes found objectionable as reflective of western paternalism and condescension, were central to our Nilotic societies. The Oxford anthropologists and their colleagues in related institutions championed them with implicit admiration as embodying principles of good governance, democracy, respect for human rights, and constitutionalism. If we observed and applied them, they could help shape an admirable model state that constructively balances unity with ethnic and cultural diversity. That was indeed what the colonial rulers did when they adopted the policy of indirect rule, which post-colonial administrations abandoned as part of colonial exploitation of culture as a tool of domination.

One of the aspects of the book which I find very attractive is his invocation of the ideals of the liberation struggle as a basis for optimistically charting the way forward:

The purpose for which we liberated ourselves from domination was to be free and build a united democratic and prosperous country for ourselves. We did not seek freedom for its own sake, but to use it as a catalyst to advance our country and bring ourselves to be counted among the best nations of this earth.

Arguing that the development of nations is never a straight line, but a zigzag, he quotes Nelson Mandela's famous saying that 'the greatest glory in the living lies not in never falling, but in rising every time we fall.' According to Lam, Mandela was talking about the power to persist in life and get up every time one falls to fight over gain. He stated:

As a people, we have come a long way to stop now. We fought for nearly a century for our freedom. We cannot look back but learn from the past and move forward. I always say that the greatest strength of the people of South Sudan during the liberation struggle was always found at their weakest point. This means that when we realize our divisions cannot serve us any better, we always unite our ranks and face challenges with herculean effort. And we have always won when we turned away from perdition.

I share Peter Lam's optimistic disposition which I frequently link to two normative principles that have always guided me in my personal and public life. One is that pessimism should be avoided as it leads to a dead end, while optimism, provided it is strategically grounded, stimulates creative and productive action. The other principle is that there are nearly always opportunities in crises and the challenge is to explore them and make effective use of them in seeking corrective remedies. Peter Lam cites the experiences of the post-war United States and the reconstruction of the European countries in the aftermath of World War II as lessons that 'should teach us that losing one's path does not signal resignation, but the beginning of developing great nations.'

Dr. Francis Mading Deng,

South Sudan's roving Ambassador and first Permanent Representative of that Country to the United Nations.

PREFACE

THE REPUBLIC OF SOUTH SUDAN came into existence through the combined efforts of military, diplomacy and citizens' decision through the plebiscite conducted in 2011. This was made possible by the Comprehensive Peace Agreement (CPA) signed by the Government of Sudan and the Sudan People's Liberation Movement (SPLM). The process to achieve independence was inclusive of all sectors and people of South Sudan from all walks of life. It is their independence! It is their country! They own it collectively! This implies that the responsibility to nurture, sustain and protect this country lies on the shoulders of every South Sudanese citizen.

However, after just two years of independence, the war that broke out in the young country became an existential threat, not only to the SPLM in which the crisis started, but also to the infant Republic of South Sudan. Though the main driver of the conflict was a power struggle between and among leaders within SPLM as to who should lead the country after the independence was achieved, certain leaders presented the problem to their people as an ethnic conflict.

For that reason, the war was fought predominantly along ethnic lines as though ethnicity were the cause. Due to this myopic view of the conflict, it was difficult for many South Sudanese leaders to remain objective and view the conflict for what it was. Instead, they considered it as war between the Nuer and Dinka which was not true. As a consequence, many South Sudanese people lost their lives believing that they were fighting an ethnic war. They did not know that they were fighting for the interest of their leaders to gain power. The worst thing was that by the time some of them realized, it was too late. The genie had already left the bottle. The country had already ignited in flames.

After the J-1[1] incident of July 8, 2016, Equatoria and Bahr El Ghazal regions became the new theatres of fighting. Once again, the war was now wrongly characterized as conflict between Dinka and other ethnic groups in South Sudan. When political leaders engage in 'telling lies' to their constituencies and they are not held accountable, innocent people die as recently witnessed in the US Capitol Hill insurrection experience which should serve as a living example for such eventuality. President Trump contended that the results of the US Presidential election were rigged in favour of his opponent Joe Biden.

However, there was no evidence for such claim and therefore, the media and the US Congress called the Trump claim as a 'Big Lie.' Through the Big Lie, five people lost their lives as the result of the brawl between the President's supporters and the Capital Hill Police.

---

1 J-1 is an abbreviation for Juba One, which is the name of the Presidential Palace in South Sudan Capital, Juba.

South Sudanese leaders who advocated and called this war ethnic knew that it was not true. They knew that such description was deceptive, yet they used it to discredit the South Sudanese body politic as a Dinka system in order to have the legitimacy to mobilize their ethnic bases for support to challenge the government militarily. As is well known, the Government of South Sudan has never been a Dinka government. It represents South Sudanese people across the world. This narrow characterization of war as being ethnic was influenced by opposition leaders, activist groups, authors of books and articles on the war in South Sudan as well as reports by international human rights and humanitarian organizations which were influenced by the agenda of the opposition political parties.

The real cause of war in the country was concealed from the people for political reasons. Even though the Nuer and Dinka murdered each other during the war from 2013-2015, not all the leaders of these two communities lost sight of their responsibility to protect the most vulnerable citizens from danger. They endeavored to preserve the unity of the people and the sanctity of the Republic. These days, authors and analysts rarely discuss what unites the people of South Sudan. It would be a fair assessment to say that since December 2013, nothing has been written about the Dinka that were protected by the Nuer and the Nuer that were protected by the Dinka.

This negligence was intentional in order to foment hatred among the people so that they would continue to fight for their leaders to gain political power. The purpose of this book therefore is to present the correct picture of this conflict as a political power struggle among elites and suggest a way forward for the country to be out of this predicament.

CHAPTER ONE

Introduction

If there is anything which characterized the majority of States in sub-Sahara Africa, it is insecurity. Since their coming into existence in the 1960s, the majority of them bore the brand of civil wars. This was because when the people of Africa fought against oppression, they came together and created a union based on their desire to be free from colonialism. The underlying cause was that colonial government was oppressive and had no regard for indigenous systems that governed traditional societies (ND shared vision, 2020; Deng, 2018). Their desire was to replace it with a system led by African leaders which would guarantee their freedom. The Africans worked under the assumption that once their liberation was completed, they would get their fair share of everything that freedom would offer.

However, when the liberation was attained and the colonial administrators were replaced predominantly with Africans, there arose a problem. The expectation of the indigenous Africans for freedom to bring about prosperity for all was not realized. Instead, they experienced an emergence of a new class of African elites who occupied the positions of colonial masters. The Africans accused their new leaders of perpetuating colonial practices of exclusion, marginalization and alienation. In affirmation to this fact, Deng (p.3, 1981) stated that:

> *Political and economic power in the hands of the nationals was viewed in collective terms not dissimilar to economic statistics of Gross National Product (GNP) which do not specify who gets what from the produce. Once the breakdown was made, inequities became apparent and just as gross statistical affluence does not gratify the poor, collective independence that gave power to a faction did not end the liberation struggle. It only changed the identities of the conflicting parties.*

As if this was not sufficient as a potential cause for trepidation, there also emerged the phenomenon of tribalism, which did not manifest itself clearly during the war against their common enemy. In fact, freedom fighters were volunteers and the question of diversity in their composition, equitable recruitment and fair remuneration which could have triggered perceptions of exclusion, marginalization and alienation were predominantly out of the equation. These fighters contributed their blood free of charge in exchange for freedom. In addition, any individual or groups of people were free to join the liberation struggle by their own volition without hinderance from any indigenous authority. Therefore, elements of favoritism or nepotism did not display themselves since there was nothing to gain in material or financial terms.

The appearance of the predicament of tribalism after independence started to threaten national unity and social cohesion within specific African countries. According to Deng (P.2, 1981):

Many African revolutionary leaders, who were guided by Pan-Africanism, disparaged the notion of ethnicity or tribes. They believed that the same unity which emerged during the war against colonialism needed to be maintained at all costs. Hence, each country utilized differing methods to deal with tribalism. In some cases, for instance, political parties that were deemed to have been formed on tribal bases were outlawed as they were viewed to promote disunity. The only acceptable option was to rally people behind one big liberation party as the only symbol of unity. For the African leaders, ethnic diversity was observed as a form of vice that threatened national independence.

The reaction of the Africans to the rule of their own children was the opposite of what their leaders expected. They fought against the same regimes they helped install to seek freedom and power from them. Sometimes, they resorted to fight for independence or more autonomy from the African ruling class (Deng, 2018; Deng, 1981).

What caused this dichotomy between African people and their leaders after independence was attained? The cause of the problem was that African leaders did not prepare their people to discuss the basis for their unity after the liberation struggle. It was assumed that the unity which was forged during the liberation struggle meant that they were united as one people and one nation. The African leaders did not realize that their unity against colonialism was based on collective interest to get rid of their common enemy. Once the enemy was gone, there was no purpose or vision to keep their unity together. The basis for becoming one people or one nation was not discussed or agreed by the Africans in their independent countries. The African leadership assumed that the purpose or vision was clear or self-explanatory to their people.

Once the realities of economic, social, and political disparity within independent African countries surfaced, discontent became inevitable. The disparities were assumed to be explained by the existence of tribalism which nurtured favoritism and nepotism in the system as some ethnic groups felt excluded from the national wealth and governance. The rest of the modern African story on governance is known...incessant civil wars.

The political and socio-economic path of South Sudan is not different from the rest of Africa. The struggle against the European colonialism gave way for independence of the Sudan in 1956. However, the fruits of that independence were reaped by the ruling elite in northern Sudan which inherited the colonial administration. In turn, the ruling class in Khartoum treated South Sudan as another colonial territory under their administration or a protectorate.

They deprived southern Sudan from provision of basic services such as mechanized agriculture, education, development of physical infrastructure, healthcare, electricity, etc. This state of affairs forced the people of southern Sudan and later joined by other marginalized people across the country to fight against the domination by the Sudanese regimes. Their struggle was manifested in various phases including the Anya Nya, Anya Nya II and the SPLM/A which signed the Comprehensive Peace Agreement (CPA) with the Government of Sudan in 2005 which provided for a referendum for the people of southern Sudan.

On July 9, 2011, South Sudan became an independent country made possible through an internationally supervised referendum in which the people of southern Sudan were allowed by the CPA to vote freely to determine their future political destiny. The euphoria of independence was felt all over the world. The international and social media carried the imagines of celebrations across the country. The unity of the people of South Sudan on that day was at its highest level.

After the Independence Day celebration, the question which dogged African countries for over half a century didn't fail to visit South Sudan. And that is the 'so what' question? The country is now independent...so what? The SPLM, like many Liberation Movements in Africa, did not ask itself that fundamental question since 2005 when it was abundantly clear that southern Sudan was going to be an independent country. It could have been logical if the ideals of the liberation struggle were recalled for implementation which according to Deng (p.30, 2018) were "Freedom from domination, recognition of their distinct culture, religion, identity, inclusivity, full equality in the governance of the country and guarantee of full rights of citizenship."

These goals of the liberation struggle were not meant to be self-fulfilling, but objectives to be realized through SPLM which is well-organized as a political party capable of 'transforming South Sudan into a democratic state. The stability of such state is to be ensured using a modernized SPLA capable of defending the territory of the young country' (Deng, 2018).

Furthermore, the SPLM did not seek the opinion of the people of South Sudan after independence to establish the basis for their unity and set national priorities to build the country for which they fought. Other political parties that existed in the Sudan and those which emerged in the country during the transitional period from 2005 were too weak to stir the nation to ask that important question as the SPLM was principally the vanguard political party that was capable of asking such a question.

Instead of thinking along those lines, the leaders in the SPLM drifted into the secondary question of leadership. Who, after independence, would lead the party and subsequently the country? Those of Dr. Riek Machar, Pa'gan Amum and Rebecca Nyandeng de Mabior began to call for President Salva Kiir, the Chairman of the SPLM, to step down as each wanted to be the flag bearer in the next election scheduled for June 2015. The 'Pa'gan Amum group' which later came to be known as Group of Ten (G-10) or Former Detainees (FDs) joined forces with that of Dr. Riek Machar and became one in their call for President Salva Kiir to step down. But their methods of taking power differed. Even President Salva Kiir made a comment after 2013 incident to one of the prominent leaders of South Sudan that, "He did not think the FDs agreed with Dr. Riek Machar and his supporters to bring about regime change through *coup d'état* in 2013" (Deng, et al., 2020, p, 157).

As a result of this dissonance within the leadership of the party, President Salva Kiir started to look for allies elsewhere to consolidate his power base. Hence, the coming into the Government of South Sudan and the SPLM those who were predominantly in the Sudanese Government during the liberation struggle. By the formation of such groupings, the trenches were dug, and war became inexorable in the young Republic. It was the question of when, not if, the war would start.

This internal squabble within the SPLM leadership led to missed opportunity for state and nation building during and after the interim period. The noble objectives of building the state and nation were set aside as power struggle within the party paralyzed the SPLM. The unity which bound the people of southern Sudan together during the national liberation struggle was assumed to continue even though the dynamics of unity changed with the independence of the country.

The dysfunction within the SPLM led to the emergence of a political vacuum which ethnic leaders had to exploit. Since 2011, the regional (Equatoria and Bahr El Ghazal) and ethnic councils (Dinka and Nuer) appeared to drive the politics of the country as the SPLM was abandoned in their favour. Even though the people of Greater Upper Nile initially resisted the idea of a regional council since the interim period, it was a singular voice in this regional political rivalry. However, in 2013, regional leaders in Upper Nile degenerated into ethnic councils as tribal connections became more important than regional unity. Thiong (2021) emphasized this point about elites pulling the country apart along ethnic lines.

As a result of the regional and ethnic rivalries, the SPLM was scapegoated. It was made to merely exist in name. The majority of SPLM members were physically in it, but their hearts and minds were with their ethnic constituencies. This situation was exacerbated by the outbreak of the civil war on December 15, 2013. The voice of the few SPLM patriotic leaders who remained committed and loyal to the unity of SPLM and the country during the crisis was overshadowed by ethnic constellations. These leaders found themselves almost incredulous, alone, and always wondering whether the leadership of the party and the government were with them in the maintenance of the unity of the SPLM and the country.

In the process, the patriotic SPLM members were sidelined and disregarded by the warring parties as too idealistic. In the words of one Dinka elder in a workshop conducted in Juba Grand Hotel in January 2014 that, 'We must build our ethnic bases first before we build South Sudan. Those of you who refuse to join your ethnic groups in favour of unity of South Sudanese are caught in a pipedream.' It was a clear blow to the Nuer SPLM cadres in government who were attending the workshop. Similar sentiments were expressed by the Nuer rebel internet warriors against the Nuer in government who were viewed to have abandoned the cause of their people in pursuit of a 'utopia' called the survival and unity of South Sudan and the SPLM. That divisive and tribal voice prevailed in 2014 as parochialism and provincialism took hold of the country.

The patriotic Nuer were viewed by the Nuer in Dr. Riek Machar's group as traitors and were misnomered as Dinkas. They gave them names like '*Nuer wew*[2] and betrayers,' as they

---

2 Nuer wew or money Nuer is a derogatory Dinka term coined by the Nuer who rebelled to describe those Nuer who remained loyal and committed to the SPLM and the Government of South Sudan

assumed that the Nuer leaders were bribed by the Dinka to stay in government and the SPLM. Some in the Dinka camp, on the other hand, saw them as Nuer self-seekers and opportunists who could have gone with Dr. Riek Machar, but for whatever reasons known only to them, remained in the government-controlled territory. Even when government reshuffles were made from 2014 to 2016, long serving SPLM Nuer cadres were not given assignments. Though they maintained their patriotic stand, they found themselves between a rock and a hard place.

There were certain leaders of the SPLM who believed that South Sudan must first be allowed to disintegrate under the leadership of President Salva Kiir. Then they would come in and re-assemble the country. This philosophy was anathema to most of the leaders in the country because of the belief that once the genie was out of the bottle, no one would be able to return it. This was because tribalism had already engulfed the country to the point where some regions no longer have the confidence to be part of South Sudan. This was clearly demonstrated by the way leaders of certain regions spoke during the national dialogue's regional and national conferences. This strategy could have fallen into the interest of ambitious political leaders who never calculate or analyze the consequences of their actions.

As the euphoria of tribalism started to dwindle in 2015, it became clear that neither side was going to win the war militarily. Many started to rationalize and joined the point of view of the patriotic South Sudanese who sought a peaceful end to the conflict in the country.

As for the organization of this book, it starts with this

---

during the outbreak of war in 2013.

introduction followed by chapter two on the birth of the Republic of South Sudan. Chapter three deals with the SPLM/A predicament from its formative years to the crisis of 2013 as well as the international influence on the need for change in the SPLM and the government. The next chapter addresses responses to the conflict by various ethnic groups and stakeholders. Chapter five puts emphasis on the mediation which includes IGAD Peace Talks and the SPLM reunification processes. The sixth chapter deals with the implementation of the Agreements through the establishment of the Transitional Governments of National Unity. The last chapter presents a way forward for the country to exit from conflict to peace and development. The chapter ends with a general conclusion.

CHAPTER TWO

―――――――

The Birth of the
Republic of South Sudan

IN THE COMPREHENSIVE PEACE AGREEMENT (CPA, 2005), an interim period of six years was provided for the Government of Sudan to make unity of the country attractive for the people of southern Sudan and other marginalized areas. This provision was important in that when the Referenda and Popular Consultations were to be conducted after the interim period, it was hoped that the likelihood for a unity vote would increase.

However, the Government of Sudan, during the CPA, did not initiate major development projects in the disadvantaged areas so as to make unity attractive. Some of the programs, such as Unity Support Fund, never buttressed any significant national development endeavor which could have altered the political views of the marginalized people towards the central government. There were no significant investments in education, health, agriculture, physical infrastructure, etc., in the peripheries of the country. In the view of many, Khartoum policy remained business as usual which was a clear indication that southern Sudan would be gone after the referendum was conducted.

Some analysts believed that the Government of Sudan understood that even if they invested in the disadvantaged and peripheral areas of the country, it could have been an exercise in futility. In their view, the independence of southern Sudan was a *fait accompli* and no national development project in that region could have altered this southern Sudanese perception.

Very few aspects of the CPA were implemented, including the formation of the Government of National Unity and the Government of southern Sudan. Others were implemented through protracted struggle, while the rest remained as outstanding issues. The Government of Sudan signed the CPA partly with the hope that it would find ways to impede its operationalization and implementation.

Outstanding issues include protocols on Abyei, Nuba Mountains and Southern Blue Nile (Ingessina Hills); border demarcation between northern and southern Sudan as they stood on January 1, 1956; as well as sharing of assets (both material and intellectual) between Sudan and South Sudan. "These national assets include: railways, Universities, public schools, Sudan Airways, oil piplines, public buildings, libraries" (ND, completing the implementation of the CPA, 2020, p.7).

The Government of South Sudan took up the issue of Abyei first as an urgent matter with the Government of Sudan. The people of Abyei were availed the opportunity through the Abyei Protocol in the CPA to choose between remaining part of the Sudan or joining South Sudan in a concurrent referendum to be conducted in Abyei in 2011. In preparation for this eventuality, a panel of local and international experts was assembled to research historical documents and interview local residents of the areas to determine whether the region was part of southern or northern Sudan. However, it is well known that the British Colonial Administration at that time annexed these area as stated below (Deng, 2020, p, 30):

> *Ngok Dinka, Twic of Bahr El Ghazal and Ruweng Dinka of Upper Nile were annexed to Kordufan in 1905 for administrative purposes and in order to provide them with better protection against Arab slave traders. Twic and Ruweng Dinka were returned to southern Sudan in the 1940s while the Ngok Dinka chose to remain under Kordofan as gatekeepers to protect the land of Dinka from Arab incursions.*

The Abyei Boundary Commission (ABC) produced a report on July 14, 2005 which was submitted to both the leadership of the Government of Sudan and the SPLM for action. The report confirmed that Abyei was part of southern Sudan.

Nonetheless, the two parties to the dispute could not agree on the implementation of the ABC report. The Government of Sudan demonized the facts in the document by presenting them to the Sudanese people as prevaricated views bent to dismember the country. Since they could not agree, the parties referred this report to the Presidency of Sudan for resolution.

This institution was composed of President El Beshir, First Vice President Dr. John Garang and Vice President Ali Osman Mohammed Taha. Once again, the findings in the report were rejected by the Presidency. Then First Vice President Dr. John Garang de Mabior was a minority in the group of three and therefore couldn't affect the decision of that institution.

Another attempt was made through the Permanent Court of Arbitration (PCA) between 2008 and 2009 to determine whether or not, the "ABC exceeded their mandate and to define the Abyei Area on the map based on the parties' submissions in the event that the Tribunal found that the ABC experts did exceed their mandate" (Kuol, et al., 2020, p.195). The final award of the Abyei Arbitration by the PCA was in favour of the Nine Ngok Dinka of Abyei. However, the award was not implemented by the Government of Sudan despite its earlier commitment to abide by the body's decision. As a result, the ABC report was destined to the shelf.

In order to procrastinate the implementation of the Abyei protocol even further, the Government of Sudan launched a scorched earth offensive against Abyei Area on May 13, 2008 and razed every hamlet and village in its wake. Most of the Abyei residents fled to the neighbouring states of Warrap, Western and Northern Bahr El Ghazal. In addition, Abyei's internally displaced persons (IDPs) sought refuge in Agok area.

This took place as an affront to the 2nd SPLM National Convention which was meeting in Juba on May 13, 2008. The discussion in the Convention on that day shifted to how the population of Abyei could be assisted and returned to their homes. Though the Government of southern Sudan and the international community managed to return home a greater portion of the population of Abyei, the Government of Sudan destroyed the area again on May 22, 2011 making it untenable for Abyei referendum to be conducted in accordance with the CPA provision.

There were some voices in the Government of southern Sudan who perceived that emphasis on Abyei issue with the Government of Sudan was going to jeopardize the southern Sudan referendum. Hence, the leaders of southern Sudan focused their energy on the success of this referendum. This strategy became one of the major criticisms of the leadership of the Government of southern Sudan and the SPLM during the interim period. Moreover, the international community also maintained a low profile on the case of Abyei. It was as though the two had a coordinated policy towards the case of Abyei.

As a result of this ambivalence, the people of Abyei decided to conduct an unofficial referendum in October 2013 in which they voted 99.9% for unity with South Sudan. The results of the vote were announced on October 31, 2013. In reaction to the referendum, only registered political parties, including the SPLM, in South Sudan recognized the results of the Abyei plebiscite. The Governments of South Sudan and Sudan did not comment on the results of that referendum. The African Union called the Abyei unofficial referendum as illegal (Sudantribune, October 28, 2013). Hence, the Abyei case remained one of the outstanding issues of the CPA (Deng, et al.; 2020; Malwal, 2017).

Nuba Mountains (Southern Kordufan) and Southern Blue Nile (Ingessina) states were accorded a separate protocol in the CPA for Popular Consultations to be conducted through their respective People's Assemblies (CPA, 2005). The purpose of

Popular Consultations was to determine whether the structures and institutions that the CPA established addressed the aspirations of the people of these areas. Modifications to the CPA structures and institutions were to be made if the results of Popular Consultations indicated any deficiencies in the way they addressed the socio-economic and political aspirations of the people of these states.

However, in Southern Kordufan and Blue Nile states, the Government of Sudan created insecurity to forestall the conduct of Popular Consultations as provided for in the CPA. In 2011, Malik Agar, Chairman of SPLM-N[3], who was also Governor of Blue Nile state and Abdalaziz Adam El Hillo, SPLM-N Deputy Governor of Southern Kordufan state were attacked and dislodged from towns by Sudan Armed Forces (SAF). This sparked the return of war between the SPLM North and the Government of Sudan.

In 2009, the African Union Peace and Security Council (AUPSC) established the African Union High-level Implementation Panel (AUHIP) for Sudan to facilitate the implementation of Darfur Peace and the CPA. After the independence of South Sudan, this panel was renamed as AUHIP for Sudan and South Sudan in 2012 to facilitate the post independence issues between Sudan and South Sudan. AUHIP was headed by former South African President Thabo Mbeki with the membership of former Nigerian President Abdulsalami Abubaker and former Burundian President Pierre Buyoya to

---

3 During the CPA's interim period, SPLM was administratively divided into northern and southern sectors. After the independence of southern Sudan, the northern sector became the SPLM North (SPLM-N).

work with the parties to the conflict to find political solutions for the new civil war both in Abyei and the two areas.

Due to political differences among the leaders of the SPLM-N and the influence of the Government of Sudan, the SPLM-N split into two groups. One was led by Malik Agar and another faction under the leadership of Abdalaziz Adam El Hillo. The latter called for referendum for the people of Nuba Mountains. Malik Agar and Yasser Said Arman (SPLM-North Secretary General) rejected this proposal by Abdalaziz. The two factions could not agree on possible reunification to face the Sudanese Government. A recent Sudanese Peace Agreement signed on October 3, 2020 in Juba between the new Government of Sudan and various opposition groups provided a glimpse of hope for peace to return to that country. Even the SPLM-N faction under Abdalaziz Adam Al Hillo and Sudan Liberation Army (SLA) under Minni Mannawi, that did not sign the Juba Agreement for Peace, have now been fully engaged by addressing their concerns in various protocols which form part of this agreement for peace in Sudan. It is hoped that their coming on board would bring peace and stability to the Sudan.

In southern Sudan, the Government of Sudan refused to demarcate the borders between northern and southern Sudan as they stood on January 1, 1956. This was an important aspect provided for in the CPA to be completed before the conduct of the referendum.

The Government of Sudan was not interested in border demarcation between southern and northern Sudan because it assumed that if borders were not demarcated, referenda in both Abyei and southern Sudan would not be conducted. However, the SPLM and the Government of southern Sudan went ahead with preparations for the referendum of southern Sudan with the support of the international community without the borders of the two regions being demarcated.

Another road block the Government of Sudan placed on the path to the conduct of the referendum was its utilization of southern Sudanese militias who were on their payroll during the liberation struggle. The objective of this policy was to destabilize southern Sudan so that referendum could not be conducted. The utilization of militias was particularly true in Upper Nile state, where they supported General Gatwech Chan, popularly known as Gabriel Tanginye, General Johnson Olony, General Yohannes Okiech and others. These militia generals were used to create instability in Upper Nile state to reduce the chances of the referendum ever taking place.

In Jonglei state, the Government of Sudan supported the forces of dissident General George Athor and General David Yauyau Jongkuch. These two Generals rebelled because they did not win seats in the 2010 general elections. In Unity state, the same government supported a group led by General Bapiny Monytuil and General Gai Yoach. In Bahr El Ghazal states, it supported the militias of Abdelbagi Ayii, Tom El Nour and others.

In the areas where the Government of Sudan could not adequately dispatch southern Sudanese militias to destroy the chances of referendum, they sent in weapons to ethnic groups to fight against each other through the new devised mechanism of '*lethalized*'⁴ cattle rustling. This was especially evident in Lakes, Warrap, parts of Jonglei, Upper Nile and Unity states.

———————————

4 The lethalized cattle rustling in this context refers to cattle theft in which owners are killed as the cattle are stolen.

Despite these political and military intrigues, the SPLM and the international community managed to bring pressure to bear on the Sudan and the southern Sudan plebiscite was conducted without borders being demarcated. The country became independent on July 9, 2011. However, non-implementation of the Abyei protocol and refusal to demarcate the borders continue to haunt both countries after the independence of South Sudan. In addition, non-implementation of the protocol on Nuba Mountains and Southern Blue Nile negatively impacts on the bilateral relations between the two independent countries.

2.1. The Pain of Divorce on South Sudan

The Republic of South Sudan attained its independence on July 9, 2011 after a protracted bloody civil war in which more than 2.5 million people lost their lives and hundreds of thousands more displaced (Both, 2003). The independence came as a result of the CPA signed, between the SPLM and the Government of Sudan in Kenya, on January 9, 2005 (Johnson, 2016). The people of South Sudan voted for independence with 98.83% in favour of divorce from Sudan.

After this historic vote for independence, the Government of Sudan applied two strategies to destabilize the young country. These strategies included creation of insecurity and application of partial economic sanctions against South Sudan.

In the sphere of security, the Sudanese Government continued to support remnants of South Sudanese militia groups that were still in its control after independence. In Upper Nile, they used General Gatwech Chan, popularly known as Tanginye. His forces fought with the SPLA in Malakal and various locations in Upper Nile until Tang and his associates were captured in the battle of Kaldak in 2011. They were put in jail in Juba and then released in 2013 just before the outbreak of war. The Sudanese Government also used the militia of General Duit Yiech and others for the same purpose.

In the Chollo Kingdom, the government utilized various commanders like General Johnson Olony and General Yohannes Okiech. General Olony fought in defense of Chollo land whom he believed was under threat of annexation by their neighbouring Padang Dinka. There were times he was used by others to fight for their causes, but only as a stratagem to get arms and ammunitions to continue his fight to defend Chollo land. Once he acquired supplies, he would revert to his original objective. At the tutelage of the Sudan Government, in an attempt to thwart the referendum in southern Sudan, he fought SPLA forces in various places in Upper Nile, including the battles of Malakal and Owachi in 2011.

The political objectives of General Yohannes Okiech were most of the times associated with those of Dr. Lam Akol who headed the SPLM–DC party at that time. He engaged the SPLA forces in northern Upper Nile with little success. Both General Tang and General Yohannes Okiech joined Dr. Lam Akol's newly created National Democratic Movement (NDM) in 2016 and were killed in Fashoda, Upper Nile state by General Johnson Olony's forces on June 4th & 7th, 2017 in Omrah and Tumur villages respectively.

In Jonglei, the Government of Sudan supported General George Athor, who rebelled in 2010 immediately after the general elections. General Athor lost the seat of Jonglei governorship to General Kuol Manyang Juuk. He ran as an independent candidate after SPLM Electoral College endorsed General Kuol Manyang as its flag bearer in the state election. The Government of Sudan supported Gen. George Athor by providing military equipment and training for his cadres until he was killed on December 20, 2011 in the border between South Sudan and Uganda by camouflaged SPLA forces posing as defectors to his movement.

In Pibor county of Jonglei state, the same government also supported General David Yauyau Jongkuch, who rebelled after he lost a parliamentary seat to a rival candidate. He got military and training support for his Cobra faction from the Government of Sudan. In Unity state, the Government of Sudan supported various militia groups, including that of General Bapiny Monytuil, General Gach Yoach and others. The same occurred in Bahr El Ghazal states where that government supported General Tom El Nour, General Abdelbagi Ayii and other groups.

Moreover, there were incidents where the Sudan Armed Forces intervened physically in destabilizing southern Sudan by utilizing ground forces and aerial bombardments from 2011–2013. This incursion into the territory of South Sudan occurred in Upper Nile, Unity, Northern and Western Bahr El Ghazal states killing and maiming hundreds of local people.

In economic affairs, the Government of Sudan was aware of the weak economic position of the young country. Basic economic commodities, such food items were not available locally in South Sudan. They were imported from neighbouring countries. The Sudanese Government decided to close all routes leading to South Sudan in order to stifle the trade between the two countries. Their hope was that South Sudan would collapse economically.

This strategy weighed heavily on the four states of Upper Nile, Unity, Northern and Western Bahr El Ghazal which border the Sudan. These states naturally depend on the supply routes from Sudan. The commodities were now to be brought from the country of Ethiopia and Greater Equatoria states which imported them from Uganda, Kenya and DRC. As a result, prices of food items skyrocketed which negatively affected the living standard of the people of South Sudan.

In the midst of all these misgivings, the Sudanese Government was enjoying the fruits of oil flowing from South Sudan. The Government of South Sudan had insufficient information on oil production as the Sudan managed the oil operations. There was no clear data on how much oil was produced per day; what the price per barrel was; to whom it was sold; what type of byproducts were produced and sold and for how much. These issues forced the Government of South Sudan to shut down oil production in 2012, when it was clear that the Government of Sudan was cheating.

When oil production was halted, the two countries suffered mutual economic hardship. As a result, they returned to the negotiation table and signed the 'September 2012 agreements' which addressed various cooperation areas. These agreements allowed for resumption of oil production and cooperation in other fields such as humanitarian affairs; opening of border routes; customs harmonization; and issuance of visas upon arrival at the ports of entry in the respective countries. However, with the exception of the resumption of the oil production, the two countries sauntered on without the implementation of these agreements.

CHAPTER THREE

The SPLM Predicament in 2013:
Implosion or Explosion

THERE IS SOMETHING to be explained about the title of this chapter. There had been semantic disequilibrium in the intellectual and academic circles to describe what happened to SPLM in 2013. Some argued that SPLM 'exploded' while others believed it 'imploded.' For semantic clarity, 'explosion' is a blast which bursts outwards whereas 'implosion' caves in.

The logic for this jargonic interplay was that when the war broke out in 2013, members of the SPLM ran in confusion. Some escaped to the bush, others were detained, and a majority remained in Juba. It looked as though members of the party ran in disarray from the center; hence, the preference for the use of the term explosion.

The second group expressed that what happened to SPLM was an ideological incongruity in which the party buried itself as an ideological organization. Since it crumbled and caved in ideologically, there was no purpose or direction which members could follow. Therefore, they argued that it was a downright implosion case.

Since this exercise is not a philosophical endeavor to dissect these two concepts *ad nauseam*, there is no need to belabour as to which term was correct to describe the SPLM perdition and predicament; but only to state that December 15, 2013 was a day when individuals in the SPLM leadership put the country at the brink of collapse regardless of the manner in which it happened.

This day would go down in history as a day when political ambition and personal greed for power almost ostensibly obliterated the young Republic for which we fought and lost millions of lives. It signaled the ultimate failure of individuals in the leadership of the SPLM to address their political differences in a civilized manner through dialogue using party structures.

Both President Salva Kiir Mayardit and his Vice President Dr. Riek Machar could have stopped the crisis before it went out of control. But they were pressed by their support bases to apply maximum herculean effort to push each other out of the ring in the party leadership rivalry, resulting in the tragedy of December 2013.

3.1 How the SPLM Got to This Point

When it comes to SPLM/A, it is an organization inherently blemished with internal leadership squabbles and infamies since its foundational years. December 15, 2013, was yet another manifestation of these tiffs, though on a larger scale. These internal clefts go back to the primordial formation of the movement in 1983 when the leaders disagreed over the leadership and the objectives of the movement.

There was an opposition group in Bilpam which declared war against the Government of Sudan in 1975 led by Commanders Vincent Kuany Latjor and Benjamin Bol Kur. Within this group were also Commanders Gordon Koang Chol, Stephen Duol Chol, William Abdalla Chuol Deng, as well as politicians including Akwot Atem. This group, which called itself Anya Nya II, had the objective of fighting for southern Sudan independence.

After the arrival of Dr. John Garang and his group to Ethiopia in May 1983, they engaged in dialogue with Anya Nya II about the leadership question and the objective of the soon to be an organized new movement. Dr. John Garang de Mabior, who would become the leader of the new movement known to be as SPLM/A, articulated unequivocally that the objective was to liberate the Sudanese people from the oppressive regimes in Khartoum and ultimately set up a New Sudan to which every Sudanese would fall heir (Khalid, 1987; Both, 2003; Nyaba, 1996; Deng, et al.; 2020).

The Anya Nya II leadership argued that Akwot Atem, who was an uncle of Dr. John Garang, would be well suited to lead the new movement given his experience and age. The group led by Dr. John Garang rejected this proposal arguing in favour of Samuel Gai Tut to be their leader with Dr. John Garang as his deputy.

The two groups differed on the leadership question but

agreed on the New Sudan vision as espoused by Dr. John Garang. However, a majority of Anya Nya II leaders and fighters thought that this objective was a strategy to gain regional and international support as secessionist movements were not sanctioned by the Charter of the Organization of African Unity (OAU).

While the two groups wrangled on the leadership question, fighting broke out between them in 1983 in which Samuel Gai Tut was killed in action and that began the litany of fighting between the two groups for almost three years. In 1987, the reunification of the two groups was initiated by then Captain James Hoth Mai, who was then the commanding officer of Yoany battalion in Kuanylou. It was only later in the process that senior SPLA officers such as David Dak Gai and Daniel Koat (D.K) Mathews and Cdr. William Nyuon Bany entered the peace negotiation and facilitated the final reunification process which was consummated in 1987.

However, this political and military unity of the two groups did not address the fundamental leadership question which split the movement in 1983. Instead, the focus of the reunification was on the need to boost their fighting capability to defeat the Sudanese Government. This historical ailment fomented another split in 1991 fitting Dr. Riek Machar's Nasir faction against the mainstream SPLM/A led by Dr. John Garang (Both, 2003; Nyaba, 1996).

The leadership of Nasir faction listed the causes of the *coup d'état* as follows (Both, 2003, pp.46-48):

1. *The state of human rights in the SPLM/A where it was accused of brutal massacre of civilians, arbitrary arrests,*

conscription of children into the army, rape, murder and looting of cattle;

2. The objective of the movement, which was the liberation of the whole Sudan, as Dr. Riek Machar put it was like chasing the moon. What the people of southern Sudan needed was to exercise their right to self-determination through an internationally supervised referendum; and

3. Lack of democracy in the movement in which all decisions were made by Chairman and C-in-C of the SPLM/A Dr. John Garang without consultation with senior leadership of the movement. They stated that there was lack of the rule of law, alienation of intellectuals and mismanagement of resources in the movement.

The SPLM/A Nasir faction under the leadership of Dr. Riek Machar championed the call for self-determination for the people of southern Sudan and other marginalized areas through an internationally supervised referendum to be conducted in southern Sudan (Machar, 1994). That call attracted many southern Sudanese members of SPLM/A mainstream to join hands with Machar in his movement.

This forced Dr. John Garang and the SPLM mainstream faction to organize the First SPLM Convention in Chukudum in 1994 which incorporated the principle of self-determination for the people of southern Sudan as one of its prime objectives. The strategy was to cater for the wishes of those southern Sudanese who were attracted to Dr. Machar's call for self-determination. As a result, many southern Sudanese who joined

Dr. Riek Machar returned to the mother SPLM/A under the leadership of Dr. John Garang.

However, inclusion of self-determination as one of the objectives of the movement did not mean that Dr. John abandoned the objective of the New Sudan. According to Deng Alor (2020, p. 54) "Dr. John Garang believed in the New Sudan vision, and he made that very clear to whoever was doubtful." He was known for saying to those who wanted to liberate southern Sudan that, 'When we liberate the territory which you believe is southern Sudan, then you can stop there, and I will continue with those who want to liberate the whole Sudan until we reach Khartoum.'

Dr. Machar and his group could not sustain their struggle independently due to lack of international and regional support. The reason for lack of interest to support him was that he led a secessionist movement, and the Charter of the Organization of African Unity (OAU) was not in favour of such movements.

As a result, they signed the Khartoum Peace Agreement in 1996 with the Government of Sudan and ultimately went to Khartoum and became part of the government system there. This was followed by the signature of the Political Charter with the Government of Sudan in 1997 in Khartoum which called for the exercise of self-determination for the people of southern Sudan through an internationally supervised referendum. The same principle was enshrined in the 1998 interim Constitution of the Sudan.

However, since the Sudanese Government-controlled Dr. Riek Machar and his group, the regime there refused to implement the Khartoum Peace Agreement. The referendum which the Khartoum Political Charter called for could not be conducted. It became tacitly clear to Dr. Riek Machar that Khartoum reneged on the agreement. As a consequence, he reconciled with Dr. John Garang and rejoined the SPLM/A in 2002 since the SPLM mainstream accepted self-determination as one of the objectives to be pursued in the negotiation of the CPA. Dr. John Garang also needed him for the success of the negotiations of the CPA in Naivasha, Kenya.

However, when Dr. Riek Machar rejoined the SPLM/A, majority of his forces remained under the control of the Government of Sudan which used them to fight the SPLM/A. Ironically, some of these forces were the ones that Khartoum used in an attempt to prevent the conduct of the referendum in southern Sudan which was scheduled to take place in 2011.

It is important here to recall that when Riek Machar returned to the SPLM/A in 2002, the reforms which he called for in 1991 were not addressed. Those contradictions remained tenacious and perhaps were deferred for future confrontation within the movement.

In 2004, a serious problem developed between Dr. John Garang and his Deputy Salva Kiir Mayardit. In addition to the rumours that he was going to be replaced with Nhial Deng Nhial in the movement, the latter believed that John Garang was using him with little to show for it. A case in point was the charge that John Garang was running the movement single-handedly without consultation with his deputy. Salva Kiir felt sidelined, guaranteed, and looked awkward among his colleagues. He believed that he was mocked and regarded by Dr. John as a nonentity (Minutes of SPLM/A Rumbek meeting, 2004).

Salva Kiir protested this treatment and consequently, a

crisis within the movement became imminent. This incident, dubbed as the 'Yei Crisis,' became so intense that it almost split up the SPLM/A once again. The causes of 'Yei Crisis' were very similar to what caused the split in 1991.

During this time in 2004, the SPLM Chapter in Canada under my leadership invited Dr. Machar to visit Canada to talk about the progress of the IGAD-led peace process in Naivasha which took more than a decade in negotiations. Dr. Riek Machar heard about this problem between the two SPLM/A leaders while he was in London preparing to leave for Canada. He called the SPLM Chapter in Canada and said that he could not make it to Canada due to a brewing predicament within the SPLM/A leadership in Yei. This forced him to cancel his trip and hurried back to southern Sudan to help address this new rupture in the SPLM/A leadership.

Dr. Riek Machar and his SPLM colleagues managed to reconcile the two men, especially in the interest of IGAD Peace Talks being mediated in Naivasha between the SPLM/A and the Sudan Government. However, even though the dis-agreement between the two men was institutional in nature, the reconciliation process was conducted as personal problems between the two leaders, as shown by minutes of the Rumbek meeting (2004). Their reconciliation did not address the institu-tional dysfunctions which brought about the trepidation in the first place between Dr. John Garang and Salva Kiir Mayardit.

During this leadership crisis in Yei in 2004, two groups emerged within the SPLM/A which were allied with each leader. Their stark differences became clear after the death of Dr. John Garang in that fateful evening of July 30, 2005 in the Ugandan helicopter crash. Speculations ran high within the

SPLM/A and South Sudanese circles as to who was responsible for the death of Dr. John Garang.

The immediate suspect was the Sudanese Government. Other suspects were the Government of Uganda, the CIA of the United States and even some personalities within the SPLM/A. Despite the investigation of the cause of death, the findings were never made public. The efforts to do so were dimmed and those involved in the investigation were gagged. In fact, Justice Abel Alier Wal Kwai, the Chairman of the Investigation Committee on the helicopter crash, was known for saying to the people with whom he talked that he would only talk about the findings of the report publicly if that would bring Dr. John Garang back to life as the risks of doing so were too great for South Sudan. Even the ghost of Dr. John Garang, in Dr. Francis Deng's Visitations (2020, p. 262), agreed "That nothing will bring me back. So, what is the point of knowing who did it and risk triggering another conflict that will lead to more death?"

3.2 Boys of Leaderships

It was often blathered about that SPLM/A leadership since time immemorial does not groom its cadres for future leadership roles. Individual members rose through hierarchy rather than on merits in the movement. One of the very few cadres that were said to have been groomed somehow for leadership by Dr. John Garang was paradoxically Dr. Riek Machar. After joining the SPLM/A in 1985, Dr. John Garang appointed him as head of SPLM Office in Addis-Ababa which was the hub for diplomatic and political activities of the party in Africa.

After he succeeded in that assignment, Dr. John Garang sent Dr. Riek Machar to command one of the largest forces in the SPLA in order to develop his military skills and capability. Had it not been for the coup of 1991 which he, with Dr. Lam Akol and Gordon Koang Chol, orchestrated, it was believed that Dr. John Garang could have made Dr. Machar his deputy in the movement, which could have brought him even closer to the center of power.

In conformity with the ordinance of the hierarchy, Gen. Salva Kiir Mayardit became the leader of the SPLM/A after the demise of Dr. John Garang. The decision to do so was unanimous in the leadership since the hierarchy was clear in the movement and the army. Salva Kiir became the Chairman of the SPLM, C-in-C of the SPLA, President of the Government of southern Sudan and First Vice President of the Republic of Sudan.

It was during this time that long held grudges and nomenclatures started to emerge in the SPLM/A. The name 'Garang Boys or Awlad Garang or more recently Garang Orphans' surfaced. Those who coined it called themselves 'Salva Boys.' The Garang Boys were mostly SPLM/A cadres who remained loyal to Dr. John personally throughout the liberation struggle and in whom he had the most trust.

The question was: who were Salva Boys? According to Nyaba (2017), this was mostly a Khartoum-based group with some SPLM/A elements from Bahr El Ghazal region whom he listed by names. Most of them were cadres who supported Salva Kiir during the 'Yei standoff.' It was this group that Nyaba (2016) accused of the ills that befell the leadership of President Salva Kiir in South Sudan since the 2005 formation of the first

Government of National Unity and that of southern Sudan.

These synthetic misnomers created insufferable feelings and rivalry among SPLM/A cadres. President Salva Kiir tried in many public fora to dismiss the existence of such political cleavage in the SPLM/A. On one occasion which I attended, he said, 'If there are people who are called Garang Boys, I must be one of them because I was always a loyal follower of Dr. John Garang.'

This political tiff between the two groups is believed to have led to the dismissal of Telar Riny Takpiny Deng and Aleu Ayieny Aleu from SPLM on November 23, 2007. Even though their dismissal was linked to the accusation that they were no longer committed to SPLM and that the two became NCP sell outs in Khartoum, they perceived this action as a political intrigue orchestrated by Garang Boys in the person of SPLM Secretary General Pa'gan Amum to distant them from Salva Kiir and the SPLM in order to control the politics of southern Sudan at that time.

In a letter dated January 26, 2008 and addressed to SPLM Secretary General Pa'gan Amum to protest their dismissal, Aleu Ayieny Aleu formally brought up the issue between the two groups of the 'Boys of leaderships' in the SPLM:

> *When we returned from Cuba after attending the political school there in 1986, you remained in Cuba to study dialectical materialism. When we arrived, our colleagues were arrested because they were accused of being progressive officers except those who were believed to have been relatives of Dr. John Garang and Salva Kiir. I was not arrested because they thought I was a relative of Salva Kiir.*

This was the origin of what is now known as "Garang boys or Awalad John." Now you falsely brand your adversaries as "Jalaba baaw" or "NCP sell outs." My dear Bolsheviks, you have won the first battle with the assistance of the unsuspecting Chairman of the SPLM whom I believe is not immune to your conspiracies. You may not be lucky in your Plan "B" otherwise; I have a strong premonition that your days are numbered in the SPLM.

When tension within the SPLM became very high, the Chairman reinstated Aleu Ayieny Aleu and Telar Riny Takpiny Deng on August 28, 2009 into the membership of the SPLM. The SPLM Secretary General was ordered to write their reinstatement letter without any investigation for their dismissal in the first place. However, the two returned to SPLM with vengeance against those they felt dismissed them from the party.

3.3 The Second SPLM Convention in 2008: When the Status Quo Saved the Referendum

The Second SPLM Convention took place in Nyakuron Cultural Centre in Juba in May 2008. There were delegates from northern Sudan, southern Sudan, and the diaspora. I was the head of the SPLM Canada delegation by virtue of being the SPLM Representative to that country. The Convention was scheduled to start on May 1, 2008 but had to be delayed until the 11th because of the SPLM internal squabbles and Darfur rebels' attack on Khartoum.

The SPLM internal schisms started to surface during the preparations leading up to the Convention. It became clear that

President Salva Kiir did not want Dr. Riek Machar to be his Deputy, nor did he want Pa'gan Amum as Secretary General of the party. According to Lual Deng (2020, p.25), "His intention was to bring in cadres who would help him in establishing a robust political system in the country through the process of political transformation." The discord sparked by this action became so acute that even those of us who came from Diaspora got sucked into it by trying to see how best we could assist our party to overcome this political impasse.

I was one of the SPLM leaders from Diaspora who considered the call for the maintenance of status quo as genuine, in order to avoid a catastrophe which was about to submerge the country. Many Dinka delegates, leaders and community elders agreed with us that the status quo should be maintained in the party in order to keep peace. Khartoum by then was working hard to plummet the SPLM into chaos by supporting certain groups in the party in the hope that this could lead to fighting between the Nuer who supported Dr. Riek Machar and the Dinka who supported Salva Kiir. Khartoum knew that fighting in southern Sudan in 2008 could have been the golden opportunity required to prevent the referendum from ever taking place.

My stand for the maintenance of status quo did not mean political support for Dr. Riek Machar and Pa'gan Amum. But my Dinka colleagues and friends misunderstood my intention because I hail from Greater Upper Nile as do those two leaders. That was why when the Liaison Office of the Government of southern Sudan was established in Canada in 2008, I was not named as the Head of the Liaison Office even though I built it from scratch as a Representative of SPLM to that country. It was a general practice at that time to appoint SPLM Representatives as Chief Liaison Officers of the Government of southern Sudan in the countries where they operated during the national liberation struggle and the interim period. That would not be the last time I became a victim for the sake of what was right. In advocating for the status quo, we wanted President Salva Kiir to peacefully lead the nation up to the conduct of the referendum in 2011.

Unexpectedly, almost all the senior Nuer politicians in the SPLM at that time supported the position advocated by SPLM Chairman Salva Kiir even though they knew that the Nuer were ready for war if Dr. Machar was relegated. And to make matters worse, the Nuer SPLM leaders did not want to provide any replacement for Dr. Riek Machar among them which could have pacified the situation when Salva Kiir decided to oust him. They also refused to tell Salva Kiir that the Nuer were ready to fight if Dr. Machar was dropped from the leadership ticket.

If I could see the problem literally upon arrival from Diaspora, why could they not see the danger while they lived with the Nuer community in Juba? In the end, the status quo became the most popular course of action and the SPLM Chairman was convinced at last to adopt it.

The second political development which delayed the Convention was Darfur rebels' attack on Khartoum on May 10, 2008. Salva Kiir was Acting President of Sudan as President Beshir went on a foreign trip. He had to move to Khartoum from Juba to handle the political situation there. The Darfur rebels penetrated deep into the heart of Omdurman and Khartoum and marched towards the Republican Palace. They were directed by their supporters in the Sudanese security forces in Khartoum. In the end, the Sudanese organized forces contained the situation and calm returned to Khartoum.

After these two political developments were addressed, the SPLM Convention started on May 11, 2008 and emerged with the maintenance of the status quo as a preferred course of action. We breathed a sigh of relief. But the success of the May Convention was at the expense of a future Convention in 2013 in that the crisis was suspended until then.

During the Second Convention, the argument was that, 'Let's keep our unity for the sake of the success of the referendum in 2011. We will make the necessary changes in the SPLM in 2013. If we want to fight, we will fight then.'

Had the status quo not been maintained, southern Sudanese hope in the referendum and independence could have been shattered. It was this deferment of reform which surfaced five years later and resulted in the crisis of December 2013. Except this time, the reform was sought by Dr. Riek Machar and his group and not President Salva Kiir.

President Salva Kiir is known for his kindness, patience, forgiveness and deliberateness in taking actions. These are his strongest qualities as leader which propelled him to lead southern Sudanese through a difficult path to referendum. These same qualities were also viewed as his weaknesses by his colleagues. His intentions were always second guessed and misread for indecisiveness and inaction by his contemporaries in the party and the government. These feelings made his comrades in the SPLM challenge him in his leadership. They believed that Salva Kiir would not take any action against them because it would pose a high security risk for the country.

As a matter of fact, President Kiir never wanted to take any action which would jeopardize the success of the referendum in southern Sudan. He knew that if the personal interest of these people was touched, they would seek military support in Sudan to dilapidate any chance for the referendum to take place. Since someone's past behavior could be a good predictor of his/her future behavior, the choice was clear for President Salva Kiir. He knew that some southern Sudanese would not hesitate to destroy the chance for independence if their personal interests were tampered with. They did it before, against the SPLM/A during the liberation struggle, and they could do it again in a heartbeat as demonstrated by some of them after the results of 2010 general elections.

After the referendum was conducted and southern Sudan was proclaimed a Republic on July 9, 2011, an important political development occurred. Independence meant that South Sudanese civil servants and politicians who were working for the Government of Sudan had to be repatriated to South Sudan. The majority of those politicians were members of the National Congress Party (NCP) of President Omer Hassen El Beshir. They were strongly opposed to SPLM/A during the national liberation struggle and throughout the interim period offered by the CPA. They used to express their disapproval of southern Sudan becoming an independent country on the Sudanese Government media. Some of them went to the extent of voting for unity in the referendum.

Because they were well trained cadres of the NCP, they knew how to attract the attention of leaders through what Nyaba (2017) described as leader worship, bootlicking and sycophancy. They managed to penetrate the weak shield of the

SPLM as a divided organization. They became close friends to the leadership of South Sudan. Nyaba (2017) further reported that they pushed away SPLM/A cadres and isolated their leader from them. It became impossible for SPLM cadres to see their leader to share with him the strategic direction of the country. And this view is shared by almost all SPLM/A cadres. As Lual Deng (2020, p.25) also gathered from the National Dialogue's grassroots consultations, "The SPLM was hijacked and rendered dysfunctional by the very people who opposed the Movement during the liberation struggle."

3.4 The Road to the December 15, 2013 Crisis

The internal squabbles in the SPLM came to a head in December 2013. However, before delving into this matter, first things first. There were quite a number of South Sudanese politicians, foreign observers and people who were frequently quoted in both the national and international media that they were surprised by the events of December 2013. There was no way those who held positions in the party, or the government could have been surprised (Young, 2019; Thiong, 2021). It was known that war was inevitable in South Sudan, but when, where, magnitude, duration and who would fire the first bullet were the only unknowns.

The issue was that South Sudanese politicians pretended that there was no problem and when the inevitable happened, they had no explanation other than to say that they were caught by surprise. It almost became a norm that facts were shunned as though people were living in an era of post-truth in the country.

If one told the truth, that person ended up with a lot of enemies in the SPLA/M system. And therefore, if somebody wanted to keep a position, the best advice given by friends was to keep quiet or despise facts like everyone else. Even elderly people, who had nothing to lose by telling the truth, choose not to speak. These prevarications caught up with the system and resulted in the December 15, 2013 crisis.

Around February 2013, the SPLM sent teams to ten states of South Sudan to seek opinions of the cadres about the performance of the party and its government since 2005. The report presented afterwards was so dismal that it shook the core foundation of the SPLM. There was no way to quibble with the facts in the report. It stated clearly that the SPLM had 'lost vision and direction'

While the leadership was grappling with the report, some senior SPLM members, especially those eyeing the top position of the party, started to connive and forestall the resultant collective embarrassment. This happened before the ossification of the report with the public in the country. In fact, many people heard about the report from the SPLM leaders who spoke and reeled publicly about it. They did not think about the inextricability of their role in the alleged failure of the party.

The public response chagrined the leaders of the SPLM who tried to distant themselves from the negative report. It was during this time that Dr. Riek Machar Teny, Rebecca Nyandeng de Mabior and Pa'gan Amum started to voice their desire to run for the Chair of the SPLM and for one of them to ultimately become the flag bearer of the party in the national elections scheduled for 2015.

3.4.1 Six Points Which Nearly Dismembered The Infant Republic of South Sudan

Dr. Riek Machar commenced to gather data for his six major political issues which he called, 'Six points of failures of Salva Kiir Mayardit' as President of the Republic and Chairman of the SPLM. He believed that Salva Kiir failed to address the following key issues: (1) SPLM's loss of vision and direction; (2) Existence of corruption in all sectors of the government and the party; (3) Tribalism and nepotism in the government; (4) Existence of insecurity in the country; (5) Economic failure as demonstrated by oil shutdown without any alternative source of revenue for the country and (6) Failure in international or foreign affairs to win friends for South Sudan.

These were the original six points which Dr. Machar presented as his platform. They were developed by and with the help of various members of a group which later came to be known as G-10 or FDs. Initially, the group involved many senior SPLM cadres, but some of them backed away from their position just before the December 6th, 2013 press confer- ence which the opposition convened in the SPLM House in Juba under the leadership of Dr. Riek Machar. The six political issues Dr. Machar raised may seem self-explanatory, but there is a need to shed light on each of them in perspective.

3.4.1.1. The SPLM's Loss of Vision and Direction

From that fateful evening of July 30, 2005, when Dr. John Garang perished in a Uganda chopper accident, the SPLM was never the same organization again. The vision of the SPLM during the national liberation struggle was to liberate the whole Sudan from oppressive regimes in Khartoum and called for the establishment of a New Sudan in which all citizens were equal stakeholders (Both, 2003; Deng, et al.; 2020). During the interim period, this vision was challenged as southern leaders turned inward to concentrate their energies on how to conduct a successful southern Sudan referendum.

By doing so, the leadership of the SPLM lost sight of the Popular Consultations for the states of Blue Nile and Southern Kordufan as well as the Abyei Area Referendum as called for in the CPA. They thought that if they didn't focus on the three areas, the National Congress Party (NCP) running the government in Sudan would soften its posture and allow them to pursue the southern political agenda with less resistance.

Since the establishment of the Government of southern Sudan (GOSS) in 2005, prominent figures of the SPLM/A were assigned to head various departments of the government, party or units of the army and other organized forces. Those who were tasked to lead the party were the Chairperson, his three Deputies and the Secretary General. The First Deputy Chairman was Dr. Riek Machar. The second was James Wani Igga and the third was Malik Agar who later became leader of SPLM-N in Sudan after independence. The Secretary General was Pa'gan Amum Okiech.

The SPLM in southern Sudan is organized from the National level to states, counties, payams and bomas. These institutions were not adequately supported financially by the SPLM National Secretariat which controlled a majority of the party's resources in those days. The National Secretariat used to send a monthly stipend of 20, 000 South Sudan pounds to each state to pay salaries of the state Secretariats but left all the lower structures without any support.

This financial constriction in the state and local levels strangled the work of the SPLM in the grassroots. As a result, there were no meaningful political engagement activities which led many to assume that SPLM was dead at the local level. It was with this understanding that when the SPLM members in the states were asked about the performance of their party in February 2013, they overwhelmingly responded that the party had 'lost vision and direction.' But in actual fact, the party lost engagement activities at the grassroots level and not its vision or direction. The SPLM vision is written and the cadres were the ones who lost sight and failed to implement it.

3.4.1.2 Existence of Corruption

Since its establishment in 2005, the Government of southern Sudan was allotted almost 50% of the oil revenues which amounted to billions of dollars during the CPA's interim period. It is incontrovertible that the SPLM/A cadres did not conduct public business in a responsible, transparent, and accountable manner. The public resources were viewed as personal and some Ministers, Chairpersons of National Commissions, Generals in the Army, and other sectors of the government and even in the SPLM were engaged in alleged financial malpractice.

And there is a philosophical underpinning for this dereliction of duty by the liberators. According to Clapham (2012), corruption usually happens to liberators in order to compensate years that were lost in poverty during the national liberation struggle. This is because of their belief that they are entitled to public resources because they liberated the country. Sometimes, they discredit the patriotism of those who did not fight directly in the liberation struggle.

Some of the trustworthy officers and politicians of the young country became affluent in a very short time. Mansions were purchased in foreign countries even as expensive homes were built in Juba in no time. The competition to get rich quickly became their preoccupation. It was clear that there was corruption in the system, but none were ever implicated or brought to justice.

As a result, South Sudan Anti-Corruption Commission was established to investigate allegations of malpractice and to refer proven cases to the then Ministry of Legal Affairs and Constitutional Development for further investigation and prosecution. However, no significant cases were ever tried or brought to book.

President Salva Kiir was very much troubled by the way his colleagues in the government and party handled public finances, but he was in a very precarious quandary. One close aid to the President explained this in exquisite detail:

> *First, the President didn't want to hold the alleged culprits to account because they could have all defected to Khartoum thereby threatening the conduct of the referendum which he passionately pursued. Second, majority of those involved in this scheme were his soldiers and SPLM comrades. He commanded them to battles and never paid them a single dime for the work they did during the national liberation struggle. If his colleagues became greedy and wanted to enrich themselves quickly, they put him in a difficult*

position to act. And finally, he thought that if they became rich, his colleagues may stop pilfering and embark on national development agenda.

Contrary to the thoughtfulness of the President, experience proves that greed produces greed, and it takes a leader to hold subordinates accountable. It was on this basis that the President issued letters to 75 senior government officials on May 3, 2012 and demanded that they return the embezzled funds to the people of South Sudan through bank accounts which were to be opened nationally and in foreign countries. It was rumored that an American advisor to the President was behind the sending of 75 letters to everyone including those who never served in the Government of southern Sudan where the crime was allegedly committed.

In his speech to the Joint Parliamentary Session on this issue, the President asked the National Assembly to help him recover the stolen funds by 75 senior government officials. The National Assembly under then Speaker Rt. Hon. James Wani Igga took the case seriously. They wanted to take tough action against those officials accused of corruption. However, the barometer of politics rose very high in Juba. Those who were served with letters became ballistic. Some of them said they were innocent while others threatened to quit the government. Another group promised dangerous reprisal against the government.

Friends and confidants went to the President and begged him to reconsider the issue as it was breaking up the government and the fragile unity of the young country. The President reversed this action in favour of stability. The National Assembly was advised not to pursue the case and that was how the issue perished. However, that action indicated that President Kiir was perturbed by the mismanagement of public resources by his colleagues in the government and the party.

Dr. Machar distanced himself from this predicament despite the fact that he was a Vice President who could have fought corruption alongside the President. He only pointed fingers at the President alone. Did he intentionally derelict his duty in order to use 'corruption' as a campaign point to discredit the President among South Sudanese who did not know the responsibilities assigned to each position in the government and the party?

3.4.1.3 Existence of Tribalism
and Nepotism in the System

Since the establishment of the Government of southern Sudan in 2005, it was contended that majority of the Ministers, National Chairpersons of Independent Commissions, Undersecretaries and any other appointed positions were occupied by the Dinka ethnic group. After fact-checking the government records, this statement could not be disputed, because the Dinka are reported to be the majority ethnic group in South Sudan and they live in seven out of ten states in the country (South Sudan Census, 2008). Since constitutional posts in the national government are distributed based on state representation rather than ethnicity, it may be the reason why Dinka get more constitutional positions in the government.

It is on this point that Dr. Riek Machar accused President Salva Kiir of entrenching tribalism and nepotism in the government. The questions which I asked Dr. Machar when I met him on May 6, 2013 were these: 'Where were you when Salva Kiir entrenched tribalism in the government?' 'What did you do as his Deputy to stop this?' His answer was that President Kiir never consulted him in his decisions. My next question was, 'Why didn't you tell the people of South Sudan that the President was working alone and appointing only Dinka people in government?' His response was that he didn't want to cause trouble and panic among the people of South Sudan. Then I followed it up with this question, 'Are you not causing trouble and panic now?' He replied, 'This is an election time, the truth must come out now.' It became clear that Dr. Riek Machar might have not said to Salva Kiir that his appointment of Dinka people into most positions of government was not acceptable in a multi-ethnic country.

Dr. Machar also bears his baggage of problems. The Nuer blame him for not nominating them for senior positions in the Government of Sudan or that of southern Sudan during the pre and post interim period. The majority of the Nuer in government were brought in by President Salva Kiir. It was alleged that those that Dr. Machar nominated for senior government positions were either his relatives or those close to him from his state. It might have been his strategy not to nominate Nuer in order for them to think that it is Salva Kiir who decided to exclude them from government. He apparently succeeded in making the majority of the Nuer feel that way.

It was reported that when President Salva Kiir asked Dr. Machar in one of the meetings conducted in J-1 in April 2013 to name a Nuer that he ever nominated for a position in government and was rejected, he could not provide satisfactory answer. This is because truth, even if it is broken into pieces and buried, has a way to resurrect and be seen.

3.4.1.4. Existence of Insecurity in the Country

From the time the Comprehensive Peace Agreement was signed by the Government of Sudan and the SPLM in 2005, southern Sudan was under constant insecurity. This was most of the times induced by the Government of Sudan to demonstrate to the world that southern Sudanese were not capable of governing themselves. They used southern Sudanese militias under their control to destabilize Upper Nile, Unity, Jonglei, Northern and Western Bahr El Ghazal states.

Almost seven out of ten states of southern Sudan were engaged in lethalized cattle rustling and inter-ethnic violence the intensity and magnitude of which was never seen before the establishment of the Government of southern Sudan. The inter-ethnic and clan fighting was fueled by weapons coming from the Sudanese Government. The main objective of their policy towards southern Sudan was that if instability could prevail, the referendum would not be conducted.

The Government of southern Sudan attempted to address this insecurity using two approaches. First, the President decided to pardon all those who took up arms against the Government of southern Sudan. By so doing, many militia commanders responded and were integrated into the SPLA with inflated military ranks including at the rank of general. He also appointed some of them into ministerial positions in the Government of southern Sudan. This attracted many of the militia commanders to respond to a general amnesty declared by the President.

The second approach was to disarm the civil population. The disarmament exercise did not yield positive results because it was not well conceptualized and organized. Certain communities were disarmed before the others. The communities that were still armed took advantage and raided the disarmed. Moreover, certain senior government officials and army generals kept re-arming their communities after the disarmament exercise. As a consequence, some communities refused to be disarmed by the government for fear of being attacked by others. This resulted in human rights abuses, especially in Jonglei state where the army was accused of excesses in the 2012 civilian disarmament campaign.

It was this insecurity that Dr. Riek Machar blamed President Salva Kiir for. Though he was his Deputy in the government and Gen. Paulino Matip Nhial (Nuer from Dr. Riek Machar's state of Unity) was also the Deputy Commander-in-Chief of the SPLA, he did not see any sarcasm with this kind of syllogism.

3.4.1.5. Economic Failure

Since the independence of Sudan in 1956, southern Sudan never enjoyed economic self-sufficiency and prosperity. The regimes in Khartoum made sure that it remained impoverished and underdeveloped for fear that an economically viable southern Sudan would pose a challenge to the northern hegemony. As a consequence, southern Sudan predominantly depended on subsistence agriculture such as traditional crop planting, cattle rearing mostly for social pride, fishing, and so forth (Both, 2003).

In addition to economic underdevelopment, the southern Sudan region was engulfed in the war of liberation for nearly half a century since the last departure of the European colonization.

When the Government of southern Sudan was established in 2005 after the signature of the CPA, the people of southern Sudan expected their standard of living to improve since the government and the resources were now in the hands of their children. Their expectations were dashed due to misman-agement of public resources and refusal to implement South Sudan Development Plan (2011-2013; 2016-2018) which set direction for the development of the country. The 50% share of oil revenues which accrued to southern Sudan Government from Khartoum desiccated in the hands of few individual leaders.

The funds were not used to develop the agricultural sector which was the mainstay of the economy in direct contradic-tion with the provisions and recommendations of the SPLM Economic Commission (2004). Against the counsel of expe-rienced economists, the Government of southern Sudan did not diversify its national economy. Revenues collected from other sources largely shriveled between the hands of the col-lectors and the institutions concerned. The country depended on oil as the only source of revenue which was detrimental to the survival of the country should anything happen to the oil sector.

In 2012, economic and political disputes arose between the Governments of Sudan and South Sudan which resulted in the shutdown of oil pipelines passing through Sudan. The world was shocked by the decision of the Government of South Sudan to do so as there was no alternative source of revenue for the young nation. However, the people of South Sudan stood by the decision of their government as they couldn't countenance Khartoum cheating them again in their independent country.

The oil shutdown dealt a staggering blow to the economy of the country. All development projects were halted as public and private expenditures were curtailed. The country now depended on revenues collected from local tax sources and imports from neighbouring countries of Uganda, DRC and Kenya which could barely pay the salaries of the civil servants.

To further deteriorate the situation, the Government of Sudan closed its routes leading to South Sudan effectively blocking all goods from coming into the country. The hope of Sudan was that the new country would collapse from this economic bottleneck. In fact, during this time, the people of South Sudan suffered greatly. It seemed as though there was never an end to the economic hardship in the country.

It was this economic constriction which prompted Dr. Riek Machar to criticize President Salva Kiir that he was not able to propose a way out of the economic decline. However, Dr. Machar was one of the politicians in the cabinet who agreed with the proposal for oil shutdown in the Council of Ministers meeting in 2012. The only politician who opposed the shutdown was then National Minister Changson Lew Chang who stated unequivocally that the country did not have sufficient reserve or alternative source of income to sustain governmental operations if oil revenues were to cease.

3.4.1.6. Failure in International Relations

There were two fundamental foreign policy issues which impelled Dr. Riek Machar to criticize the President. One was an incident with the UN Secretary General Ban Ki-moon with regard to the battle of Heglig. The other was related to

President Barack Obama of United States about SPLM/A-North's military activities in the Sudan.

Throughout the interim period, the Government of Sudan intermittently bombarded the northern states of southern Sudan in various locations both by air and on land. These violations were reported to the United Nations several times. However, there was no action or word of condemnation of the Sudanese Government by the world body.

On April 10, 2012, the Government of Sudan attacked SPLA in Kharasana, northern part of Unity state. As the battle intensified, the Sudanese Army retreated as SPLA pursued them to their base in Heglig where their trenches were overrun. Encouraged by their unprecedented victory, the SPLA chased them out of Heglig and encamped in their base. This all happened without any knowledge of the President (Deng, et al., 2020; Deng, Lual, 2020). He was informed later after the fact by then SPLA Chief of General Staff Gen. James Hoth Mai. The reason was that the SPLA forces who captured Heglig did not actually know that they reached that area until they got confirmation from their commanders. This was because Heglig has the same geographical terrain like South Sudan and most of the solidiers deployed there had never been posted to that location before.

The fall of Heglig (Panthou) sent shock waves throughout the Sudan and the world to the point that then Secretary General of the United Nations Ban Ki-moon called President Salva Kiir by phone to immediately withdraw the SPLA forces from Heglig.

This order did not sit well with President Kiir who got frustrated by the inaction of the United Nations whenever South

Sudan was attacked by Sudan and the organization turned a blind eye to the people of South Sudan. Kiir said to Ban that it was the Sudan Government which attacked South Sudan first and that SPLA forces would withdraw, but at their own pace. This conversation created misunderstanding between the two leaders.

Ban Ki-moon henceforth developed negative attitude towards President Kiir and this was reportedly leaked to then Vice President Dr. Riek Machar by western diplomats stationed in Juba, including senior UN officials working in South Sudan. He used this information as an opportunity to criticize President Salva Kiir in his handling of foreign relations.

The issue with President Obama related to South Sudan's alleged support to the SPLM/A-North. The SPLM/A-N scored victories against the Government of Sudan in both Southern Kordufan (Nuba Mountains) and Southern Blue Nile (Ingessina) states. The Sudan and the world believed that the SPLM/A-N opposition was assisted by the Government of South Sudan, since they were part of the mother SPLM/A before the independence of South Sudan.

In accordance with the provisions of the Comprehensive Peace Agreement (CPA), the SPLA-N could have been in-tegrated into the Sudan Armed Forces (SAF) before the ex-piration of the interim period. However, the Government of Sudan was not willing to do so. As a result, when Popular Consultations were not held in the two areas as stipulated in the CPA, war broke out again in the Sudan. The Government of South Sudan and the SPLA insisted that they did not provide any assistance to SPLM/A-North.

It was in line with this issue that President Obama spoke

with President Kiir about this alleged support to the rebels of the Sudan. When President Kiir said to President Obama that his government did not support the Sudanese rebels, Obama was not impressed because he had evidence (Edwards, 2016). He believed that Kiir did not tell him the truth. In fact, he confronted Kiir with satellite imagery which showed certain black soldiers wearing SPLA uniform crossing into the Sudan. He considered those soldiers to be from the SPLA-South Sudan.

President Obama felt that he was deceived. Though President Salva Kiir wrote a letter of clarification to Obama after this episode, the US President already felt deceived and had taken a stand against South Sudan government led by President Salva Kiir.

Hence, Vice President Dr. Riek Machar utilized this exchange between the two leaders as yet another means with which to hit out against President Kiir in his way of handling foreign affairs. The apparent question was, if the President was not aware of any support to the Sudanese opposition by his government, why would he give in to international pressure and accept something which did not reflect the reality in his country? The people of South Sudan would have liked to hear how Dr. Machar would have responded to these allegations by foreign powers which were denied by the government in which he was the Vice President.

In summary, it was not fair to blame President Salva Kiir as exclusively responsible for all the problems that happened in South Sudan and the SPLM as the ruling party during the transitional period and immediately after independence. The SPLM leadership in totality was responsible for the failures which Dr. Riek Machar listed. As Lual Deng (2020, p.16) observed, "The three leaders of the SPLM (President Salva Kiir, Dr. Riek

Machar, and Pa'gan Amum) were equally responsible for the drivers behind the six symptoms of South Sudan's malady. This is because they were all in government and SPLM during the period from August 2005 to July 23, 2013."

3.4.2 The Campaign for President Began

Former Vice President Dr. Riek Machar launched his campaign by utilizing the six political issues stated above from February 2013 onwards. He commenced this by calling group meetings in his residence to present his position on these issues. First, he started with his close friends who supported him during Khartoum Peace Agreement of 1996 and Political Charter of 1997. After that, he extended his invitation to certain Nuer members of the National Legislature (National Assembly and Council of States). Then he targeted other Nuer in the executive branch of government whom he knew would support his bid for President. He courted the Nuer local chiefs in the counties of Upper Nile region to support him as well as appointing others to act as focal points in some state governments to coordinate and mobilize support for him.

He effectively utilized the Churches in Juba to explain his political platform on Sundays. This was where he used the famous phrase, 'It is time for Nuer to eat.' In all cases, he outlined the failures of President Kiir using his six political points mentioned earlier. He believed that he was the only one who could correct those failures in the system. Then he would end with an appeal to the congregation to support his ticket to ascend to the top leadership of the SPLM and subsequently the President of the Republic.

Dr. Machar's wife, Angelina Nyajany Teny, also started to campaign by mobilizing Nuer women and youth to support her husband's bid for President. In March 2013, she formed what came to be known as 'Naath Youth for Change.' The objective was for the youth to mobilize the Nuer in urban areas and villages to support the ticket of Dr. Machar in the upcoming elections.

The idea that Dr. Riek Machar could become the next President of South Sudan was a welcomed proposal by the Nuer community all over the world. They started to pour in their moral support to the man through phone calls and visits to his office and residence. A majority of South Sudanese also started to view him as a formidable presidential contender although for a different reason from what the Nuer thought. In fact, Dr. Machar had many supporters in Lakes, Northern Bahr El Ghazal, Greater Equatoria and Greater Upper Nile states. From political perspective, he was in the offing, in fact, was gaining considerable acclaim as a candidate.

The Bor Dinka community of Jonglei state, which held grudges against him for the massacre of 1991, started to court him politically. Dr. Riek Machar also sought this community for political support. The two interested parties met in the middle of the road. This change of heart was said to have been facilitated by a senior politician in that community.

On August 28, 2011, while marking the 20th Anniversary of Nasir Declaration, Dr. Machar apologized for the Bor Massacre of 15 November 1991. He did so again during a community reconciliation workshop conducted in Bor on April 4, 2012 (Sudantribune, April 4, 2012). This was where he apologized copiously to them for the atrocities committed against their community in 1991. In fact, it was reported by those present that Dr. Riek Machar wept in contrition. Everyone familiar with Dr. Machar knows that he rarely indulges in emotional catharsis in heart-wrenching circumstances. The occasion must have meant a lot to him. The Bor elders in that workshop all talked in conciliatory tones and forgave him for the 1991 carnage. Some of them, however, hinted that for the apology to be meaningful, Dr. Machar should do so to the entire community in Bor town, rather than in the confines of a conference hall.

The Nuer community in Juba was flabbergasted and confused by what happened. They asked questions like: Why would Dr. Machar apologize to Bor community? Did he order the killing of Bor people in 1991? Has he been denying it all this time and only to admit it there? Only Dr. Riek Machar has answers for these questions. What is known is that the Bor community is one of the strongest political centers in South Sudan and their support would give him a very high political clout as he sought support for his ticket. It was therefore reasonable for him to reconcile with them.

While all these activities ensued, some of the Nuer people in Juba and all-over South Sudan began to talk carelessly about fighting the Dinka and taking power from them by means of arms. This was done in conversations in restaurants, tea places, domino playing areas, as well as churches. In fact, the Nuer churches became the places where priests and pastors allowed politicians to present their programs clearly fraternizing the roles of Christ and traditional prophecies.

While the Nuer were talking carelessly about the war, the Dinka were listening to what was being said. No one knew what the Dinka were planning to do as they were subtle and airtight. In the African Union Commission of Inquiry Report (AUCISS, 2014) and the book by Edwards (2016), it was alleged that there was an informal structure established to respond to this Nuer overture.

In late April and early May 2013, the tension between President Salva Kiir and Vice President Dr. Riek Machar came to a head. In April 2013, the President issued two edicts. One was for withdrawal of Presidential powers delegated to the Vice President. The second was to relieve Vice President Dr. Riek Machar as the Chairman for Peace and Reconciliation process as well as abolish the process itself. The Vice President was accused of using this process as a forum to discredit the President as he campaigned for the top job. In fact, Dr. Machar on more than one occasion used the process to talk about the failures of the Government of South Sudan under President Salva Kiir.

The politicians and elders of the four districts of the Nuer community realized that the political gap between the two men widened to the level of crisis and that there was a need to discuss the way forward with the President and his Deputy. The strategy was for Nuer community of Bentiu, Lou, Fangak and Eastern Jikany to meet with the two leaders separately.

The main message was that there was a need for the two leaders to discuss their differences and reconcile so that the communities of Nuer and Dinka were not antagonized. I was one of the 40-member delegation from Eastern Jikany who attended the meeting with the President on May 1, 2013. We were the last Nuer community to meet and present our Petition to the President which contained the following points:

1. *That the brewing problem in the country was an SPLM problem which must be discussed and resolved within the SPLM Party structures as it pertained to leadership of the party;*

2. *That the SPLA must not be involved in the political wrangling within the SPLM to support any of the leaders;*

3. *That the civil population (Nuer and Dinka) need not be mobilized to get involved in the SPLM political crisis;*

4. *That the President had the right to rescind powers he delegated to the Vice President because this was in line with his constitutional powers; and*

5. *That the President and Vice President needed to jointly hold a press conference and address the nation to demonstrate unity in the country.*

After the presentation of the Petition to the President, five people were asked to speak. In my strongly worded statement, I was clear that Dr. Riek Machar was wrong to criticize the President while he was still Vice President. However, I advised the President that he should not relieve Dr. Machar as Vice President. I didn't elaborate on this, but I thought it was tacitly clear. When I said this, the President raised his head and made eye contact suggestive of a decision already contemplated although not yet taken. I had hoped that he would change his mind because I knew what that would mean for the country in terms of peace and stability.

The supporters of Dr. Machar in our group all looked at me in awe. In fact, they turned from their chairs to look behind where I was speaking because they did not expect this since it was known that I supported the President. But when their turn came to speak, they cowed to say anything that would be deemed as an affront to the President because some of them held senior positions in the government at that time.

When we left the meeting hall, I was stopped by journalists to brief them on the meeting we held with the President. I hesitated to talk because the right person to speak to the press on this matter was David Koak Guok, the Jikany Nuer community Chairman, who was by then the Chairman of Local Government Board. They informed me that David already gave them a statement, but they needed my perspective. Being a former Minister of Information and Broadcasting in Upper Nile state, they knew me well as we had developed friendship over the years.

I obliged to their request and enumerated to them the points in our petition to the President. I knew those were the same issues that David talked to them about. However, one journalist asked me this question, 'What caused this problem which you say should be discussed within the SPLM structures?' The answer to this question became pivotal in my relationship with the group of Dr. Machar for the rest of the ensuing political developments in the country. My response was that 'We have a crisis in our hands because the Vice President has declared to run for President before the election time.'

That evening, I was inundated with phone calls from supporters of Dr. Riek Machar all over the world condemning and intimidating me for saying that. Some calls came from Ethiopian Nuer in Gambella region while others came from Canada, USA, and Australia. Other phone calls were from those who attended the meeting with me. They said that my statement was not part of the points enumerated in the petition to the President. I did not know how else I could have described the problem without naming the root of the issue.

It was only then that I realized the political network and mobilization which Dr. Machar already made was wide and sophisticated. In fact, the late John Chuol Char and Gatluak Riek Jaak, both MPs in the National Assembly, and Lam Chuol Thichuong, Private Secretary of Dr. Riek Machar, not only called me that evening to express their anger but became so concerned that they went to the media the next day to negate my statement. They said that Dr. Machar did not vie for the position of President and that I had deceived the people of South Sudan. It was their considered position that there would be no war in the country because of this issue.

I expected David Koak and Wiu Kun Kuiyang to react to my interview as they were the leaders of Jikany community in that meeting. But they became silent for reasons known to them. Maybe their feelings were expressed by their colleagues who criticized my statement in the media. Because all I said turned out to be true in December 2013, I sometimes joked with those MPs that they owed me a public apology since they rebuked me in public.

On May 4, 2013, we met Vice President Dr. Riek Machar in his office to submit to him the same petition we presented to President Salva Kiir. At the first sight, the number of our delegates increased from forty who met with President Salva Kiir to more than sixty people. The meeting atmosphere was tense and unfriendly. It became clear from our meeting with the President that we had two groups; one supported the President and the other his Deputy.

Therefore, the leadership of Jikany community replaced the supporters of the President and precluded them from speaking. For that reason, they replaced me along with other like-minded colleagues while they allowed those who supported Dr. Riek Machar to speak.

However, before they could finish talking in that meeting, Dr. Machar interrupted the person who was speaking to say that our points in the petition were clear and self-explanatory and that it would be good if we could hear from him. He seemed briefed in advance by his supporters about what transpired in our meeting with the President. He also wanted to convince those who were not for him to change their mind by listening to his point of view on this important matter.

He agreed with all our points in the petition except the last one which stated that they should go to the media and make a joint press conference to address the nation. He said that if they addressed the nation together, it would send a wrong message. In his view, there was no problem in the country. He said, 'This is a democratic country and I have the right to speak about what I want.'

In that meeting, he declared his desire to run for President based on the points he enumerated as failures of the President. He challenged all of us who disagreed with his position to state why. Those of us who had issue with his line of thinking were poised to challenge him. However, as soon as he finished talking, the leadership of Jikany community decided that they would not allow any debate. They only allowed then Minister Changson to thank the Vice President for giving us his time to meet him.

That was the end of it. After the meeting, Dr. Machar and his supporters in the meeting went for a group photo and those of us who were not on his side didn't even know that there was a photo opportunity priorly arranged.

On May 6, 2013, a meeting between me and the Vice

President was arranged by Miyong Gatuor Kuon, who was one of his media aides. Miyong is from Ulang county as I am. He was concerned that I became the subject of discussion in the office of the Vice President. They said that I betrayed the cause of the Nuer because I did not support Dr. Machar's bid for President. Since we both come from Ulang, I guess he was probably brushed by his colleagues in their comments against me. It concerned him to the point that he requested Dr. Riek Machar and I to meet and discuss the matter.

Therefore, on Monday May 6, 2013 at about 4:35pm, I met with Dr. Riek Machar in the presence of his aides, including the late Lam Chuol Thichuong, Miyong Gatuor Kuon and his Press Secretary James Gatdeet Dak. As soon as I entered his office, the Vice President stood up, performed perfunctory greetings and asked me to tell him what I said to the media that embittered the Nuer people all over the world.

While still standing, I restated the statement I made to the media that, 'The reason why we have a crisis in our hands is because the Vice President has declared to run for President before the election time.' He was surprised and said, 'If this was what you said, then you are right. I am running for President.' He looked at late Lam Chuol Thichuong and said, 'Didn't I tell you to inform our people that I am running for President? Why do you say that Peter Lam Both said something wrong?' Chagrined, Lam Chol looked down in shame. I could have asked Lam Chol to repeat what he said to me on the telephone on May 1, 2013 when he reacted to my statement, but I didn't find him worthy of the time.

Dr. Riek Machar went back to his seat and invited me to sit so that we could start the discussion. He explained why he was determined to run for the position of Chairman of SPLM and ultimately the position of the President of the Republic.

My response to his presentation was that he was wrong. He was visibly perturbed by my answer. That did not deter me from the opportunity of telling him in earnest my thoughts about the matter. I explained to him how he was at the center of the failures he presented as failures of the President.

First, I validated his theory that there were six or even more points of failures of the government and the SPLM, but I argued that those were collective systemic failures and not mistakes of any particular individual in the system like the President. In this scenario, I gave him the opportunity to disentangle himself from these failures notwithstanding the fact that he was the Vice President of the Republic and First Deputy Chairman of the SPLM. I was a member of the SPLM National Convention with a vote to cast for or against any of the aspirants of the top positions in the SPLM. It was necessary for him to convince me with reasons. In my view, his response to my question was amiss.

My final thoughts to him on this matter were that 'You have smothered both Kiir and yourself, risking political banishment by the people of South Sudan in the forthcoming 2015 general elections. You have given them ammunition against both of you in the ballot box. You cannot escape from this blame. You have dug your political graves.'

Secondly, in February and March, Dr. Machar engaged the Nuer in several meetings at his residence to support his bid for President. This political development in the country was viewed as a Nuer tribal stratagem to snatch political power from the Dinka. I encouraged him to abandon the utilization of a tribal card in the politics of South Sudan as it didn't help him in his

1991 bid for the same position. Besides, many of his colleagues in the SPLM/A think that he was responsible for planting the seeds of tribalism in the SPLM/A. In the words of Deng Alor (Deng, et al., 2020, p.59), "This idea of tribalism really started to come up in the SPLM/A with Dr. Riek Machar. He was the first to introduce this concept of Nuer versus the Dinka which he pursued aggressively up to the Bor massacre in 1991."

To demonstrate this point, a cartoonist by the name of Adija Acuil drew a caricature of Dr. Riek Machar in the Citizen Newspaper in April 2013 standing with a stick pointing at a group of South Sudanese and asking them which tribes they belong. With their hands up in the air, they responded that they are South Sudanese. For the Vice President to be depicted as tribalist in a caricature was detrimental to his bid for the top job in the country.

There was no considerable evidence that the tribal card would work for him this time. He needed the support of other ethnic groups in the country if he wanted to be President. Though the Nuer vote was important, it would not *en solo* bring him to the Office of the President. Therefore, my advice to him was that he needed to present himself as a national leader for all South Sudanese. He needed the support of all the people if he wanted to be President of this country.

Thirdly, Dr. Riek Machar had the support of many senior officials from Dinka and Equatoria communities for reasons that might not have been genuine. I was astonished by their unprecedented support. While I was in the reception of the Vice President's Office waiting to be called in for this meeting, one businessman from a certain Dinka community was also waiting with me there. He was playful with the staff of the Vice

President saying in Arabic Juba, *"Lou Dr. Riek Machar ma yekun raise fi fatera da, kali shakla ye gum beyna Nuer wu Dinka."* This roughly translates that if Dr. Riek Machar does not become President this time, let fighting start between Nuer and Dinka.

I was very much disgusted and perturbed by this statement, but I did not want to respond to a stranger. I mentioned to Dr. Machar in this discussion that he needed to be wise. Some leaders from Dinka community wanted to push him out of the SPLM by giving him wrong advice. I informed him about the statement of that businessman. I said to him that he should ask that man for me this question: When the Nuer and Dinka fight, on whose side will he be?

Fourth, Dr. Riek Machar had a perennial problem with the Nuer politicians and intellectuals. He considered them as potential political rivals and therefore seldom engaged with them on issues of leadership and governance in the country. They accused him of not supporting them to get senior government positions. From 2005-2013, Dr. Machar rarely nominated any of the Nuer for senior government positions. If any, his known nominations in the Nuer community largely included his relatives and those from his state.

His critics often said that he sometimes hoarded positions for himself at the expense of other eligible Nuer leaders. For instance, when the Government of southern Sudan was formed in 2005, Dr. Machar held three positions: Vice President of the Government of southern Sudan, Minister of Housing and Public Utilities and MP for Leer County. He could have given away the Ministerial and MP positions to his supporters who did not get anything in the government. Consequently, his longtime supporters who were with him in South Sudan

Independence Movement (SSIM) found themselves in the cold. He seemed to have forgotten the cardinal rule of politics that you 'sccratch my back and I will scratch yours.'

When he was planning his political strategy to oust the President, he informed very few Nuer politicians, intellectuals and senior government officials. He eschewed them and looked for soft targets that would agree with him without any critical analysis of the consequences of his actions.

The Nuer politicians and intellectuals also held low opinions about the leadership capability of Dr. Riek Machar. He demonstrated poor judgement as a leader when he fractured the SPLM/A in 1991 which resulted in the Bor massacre as well as the internecine Jikany-Lou conflict which lasted for many years (Both, 2003).

As a result, territories that were liberated were retaken by the Sudanese Government because of the disunity that the split brought. In the words of Dr. John Garang, 'These people will be remembered for stabbing the movement in the back when we were at the point of winning.' Moreover, after signing the 1996 Peace Agreement with Sudan Government, he went to Khartoum and left all his forces there when he decided to re-join the SPLM/A in 2002.

Dr. Riek Machar believes that his power will come from the Nuer civil population and the prophecies of Ngundeng which in most cases were distorted by certain individuals to suit his cause. As a consequence, he consistently maintained good relations with Nuer local Chiefs and elders whom he believes would mobilize people to vote for him. This seems to be a wise move from the surface. However, beneath the connivance, those elders are mothers and fathers of the Nuer politicians and intellectuals. And they could turn them against him any time should that be necessary. I stated to him that he would not be what he aspires to become without the support of the Nuer intellectuals and politicians.

Fifth, endorsement and support of President Salva Kiir was critical for him to become President of South Sudan. Without any circumlocution, I said to him that he needed Salva in order to become President. He squinted his eyes and became restive in skepticism and asked me to explain why I gave such a power to Salva Kiir. I recalled for him the scene of the 2nd SPLM Convention held in Juba in May 2008.

Before the Convention took place in May 2008, Salva Kiir made it clear that he did not want Riek Machar to be his Deputy and Pa'gan Amum to be SPLM Secretary General. Up on hearing these rumours, I and some delegates from Canada and United States went to the house of Dr. Machar to confirm if the rumours we heard were true. We arrived at his residence around 1:00am in the morning.

He was at home with his wife Angelina Nyajany Teny sitting in the living room. I asked him about the issue. He confirmed that the rumor was true and that he decided to contest for the Chair of the SPLM against Salva Kiir. My next question was whether he prepared himself for this as no one ever heard him declare interest to compete for the top position. He said he was going to start the campaign that night. His wife held the same views and agreed with his plan to run. I wondered how they could win an election that they did not plan and campaign for literally over night.

I revealed to them the plan we came up with as delegates. We proposed to maintain the status quo in the party. He was doubtful pointing to the obvious fact that Salva Kiir would not accept such a proposal. I responded that the electorate was stronger than Salva Kiir and whatever the majority of voters decided, would carry the day in the end.

We departed from his residence. The next morning, we went to Pa'gan Amum and gave him the same message. We found him so distraught that he was prepared to leave for the United States where his family was. He almost gave up any hope. I told him that we were going to bring him back as Secretary General and that this was a matter bigger than one particular person. I assured him that we would resolve the problem without invoking ethnic affiliations. He agreed to postpone his journey.

We had to mobilize the delegates to the Convention and explained to them the importance of keeping the status quo for the sake of peace in our country. The delegates from Bahr El Ghazal understood this strategy very quickly and began to campaign for it. What was at stake at the time was the referendum because conflict was imminent between Nuer and Dinka if Dr. Riek Machar was not brought as Deputy Chairman. It was clear during the consultation meetings held in Juba that the Nuer were ready to fight if Dr. Machar didn't make it. If such conflict happened, the referendum could have been lost and we were not prepared to risk such a ubiquitous national objective.

After a protracted persuasion by the delegates, especially elders and delegates from Bahr El Ghazal, President Salva Kiir agreed to keep the status quo. For the first time after many postponements, the Convention started on May 11, 2008.

During the Convention, something extraordinary manifested

itself in the Hall of Nyakuron Cultural Centre. If any leader of the SPLM entered the hall, the Convention delegates stood up and clapped for him/her. However, whenever Dr. Riek Machar came, only Nuer delegates from the states of Upper Nile, Jonglei, Unity and Diaspora would stand up and clap for him. It was a clear indication that Dr. Machar was in political turmoil. But, when the strategy to keep the status quo was adopted and Chairman of SPLM Salva Kiir nominated Dr. Machar for the positon of First Deputy Chairman, he was elected by acclamation. No one opposed his candidacy because Salva Kiir nominated him. He couldn't have won if Salva Kiir didn't nominate him.

I brought this up in my meeting with him because he seemed to have forgotten that Salva Kiir could still endorse him to become SPLM Chairman and none of his political opponents would stop that. That was what I meant when I said he needed Salva Kiir in order to get the top post in the country.

Sixth, I submitted to Dr. Riek Machar that it was too early to talk about elections in May 2013 when the national elections were scheduled for June 2015. The 3rd SPLM Convention was supposed to take place in May 2013, but because of the dissonance within the SPLM Political Bureau, the Convention was delayed.

The basic documents of the SPLM such as the Constitution and Manifesto were in draft forms and consultations with grass-roots were not yet completed. It is only after these documents were finalized and endorsed by Extraordinary SPLM National Convention that the campaign to fill party positions would begin.

Instead, Dr. Machar started his campaign early in February 2013. I told him that this early campaign would make it difficult to draft the basic documents of the SPLM with honesty because, 'each of you would want drafts to be reflective of your individual interests in the party.'

Finally, I raised the context of South Sudan as a country in relation to western democracy. Our nascent nation was too young and inexperienced to face high political turmoil and shocks. The concept of western democracy, which is constantly misunderstood in Africa, has not yet crystalized in the minds of our ethnic groups. Our people follow leaders not because they agree with them substantively, but because they come from the same ethnic background.

Any political rivalry between Dr. Riek Machar and President Salva Kiir would be perceived by Nuer and Dinka as an ethnic divide, and this would throw the country into political turmoil. I argued that this would trigger the repeat of 1991 with severe consequences because one group would now be the government and in possession of national resources. Hence, the Nuer would suffer as a consequence if war broke out.

I submitted to Dr. Machar that it was necessary to educate our people first about what modern western democracy is and its inherent responsibilities. Once such civic education has taken place, then elections and peaceful transfer of power would be possible. Otherwise, our people would be destined to die again as they did in 1991.

William Deng Deng, then Chairman of South Sudan Disarmament, Demobilization and Reintegration (DDR) Commission also held similar views and addressed Dr. Riek Machar in April 2013 in a letter making the same point about the consequences of the application of premature western democracy in an ethnically divided country. He wrote:

Democracy in South Sudan is still ethnicity based rather than on merits of Presidential candidate's manifesto. There is a dire need for sustained widespread civic education of the general population about democracy and what it truly means for an ethnically diverse country like South Sudan. We saw in the last elections (2010) that candidates that lost in their contest for political office started a rebellion which cost the nation lives and wasted resources in ending it. Given that you are a Nuer and Salva Kiir is a Dinka, the potential split of these two groups and the attendant tension and conflict will not serve our ethnic or national interest. The fighting between these two groups will snowball and undermine national reconciliation, healing, and unity which we have been trying to achieve.

The advice from the two of us to Dr. Riek Machar was similar to what then British Prime Minister Tony Blair said to Deng Alor in the form of admonition for officials of the new Government of southern Sudan (Kuol, et al., 2020, p.56) that:

Western democracy evolved over time. There were wars and dictatorships until we reached the stage we are at now. For you, you don't need to embrace the current Western democracy overnight. Singapore for instance has gone from a very poor highland to one of the most developed countries in the world in 30 years. An economic vision and strong hand made Singapore what it is today. We differed with Lee Kuang Yew over his dictatorial style, but he led his country to development.

However, Dr. Machar held a different perspective on this issue. He was determined to challenge the President and was not ready to change his mind for potential consequences of his action. He only said that there was no time set for democracy to take hold in South Sudan and that it was time to start the exercise of democracy. He blamed me for trying to buy more time for Salva Kiir to stay in power and that my concerns, though genuine, were not persuasive enough for him to stop what he planned to do.

After this deliberation, I asked him one last time, 'Dr. Machar, do you really want to be President of South Sudan?' He answered me in the affirmative. I said, 'If that is the case, please change your strategy. You need to be strategic because the approach you want to use would not carry the day unless you have another plan. It is known that this strategy proved unproductive in the erstwhile. This time, you need to be a different politician. If this political power struggle led to war between Nuer and Dinka, your political career will have ended.' In response, he said, 'I would not tell you if I had another plan because you will reveal it to President Salva Kiir.'

After this, he asked his Press Secretary James Gatdeet Dak if he had written all the issues I presented. James Gatdeet's answer was negative. Then he asked me to give him my notebook so that his Press Secretary could copy. I did so without any hesitation. He promised me that he would think about what we discussed. We ended our meeting around 6:00pm and I went home straight from there.

In the evening, someone told the President that I met Dr. Riek Machar, and he called me at 11:00pm. I was almost asleep. I picked up the phone and we talked. The reason for his call was to brief him on the outcome of my meeting with Dr. Machar. I turned on the light and I read to him the points I just enumerated. His reaction was that I almost made him President if only he could listen to my advice. He further stated, 'But I know my brother Dr. Riek Machar, he cannot listen to anyone. He knows everything. However, congratulations for your advice to him.'

3.4.3 International Influence on the Need For Change in the SPLM and Government

The international community was bewildered by the unexpected demise of Dr. John Garang de Mabior on that unfortunate evening of July 30, 2005. They wondered whether the Comprehensive Peace Agreement (CPA) which the SPLM concluded with the Government of Sudan would hold after his passing.

However, the leadership of the SPLM did not loath to appoint Gen. Salva Kiir Mayardit to succeed Dr. John based on his seniority in the SPLM/A. This decision was hailed throughout the world. Salva Kiir promised that the SPLM had no reverse gear and that it would implement all the necessary provisions of the CPA to the letter with the Government of Sudan.

In fact, the people of South Sudan likened the death of John Garang to the story of the children of Israel when Moses died, and Joshua took over the leadership and led them to the Promised Land. Indeed, Salva Kiir was dubbed as, 'The Joshua of South Sudan,' a phrase which an officiating pastor uttered at the funeral of Dr. John Garang.

The Troika (United States, UK, and Norway), European Union, African Union and IGAD were pleased with the political path South Sudan leadership took to implement the

CPA. It was clear that they would back the conduct of the referendum as they saw the leaders of South Sudan demonstrating political maturity in how they handled the affairs of the state after the passing of their leader.

However, as time went by, the international community came to the realization that the leaders of South Sudan had challenges with good governance, especially in the realm of financial architecture, management, and democracy. They exerted extreme pressure on the leadership, especially on the President of the Government of southern Sudan, to punish those responsible for embezzlement of public funds.

The first sign of corruption was reported on the 2nd Anniversary of the CPA in 2006 when President Salva Kiir accused President Beshir of Sudan at a podium as they addressed the Sudanese people from Juba. President Salva Kiir stated that the Sudanese Government had not released funds to start recovery work in southern Sudan.

Surprised and shocked, President Beshir responded angrily that the Government of the Sudan gave $60 million dollars to the leaders of southern Sudan to start-up government institutions and to bring qualified southerners from Diaspora to help jump-start development in southern Sudan.

Almost all the people of southern Sudan were stunned by this statement including President Salva Kiir. Majority of the people in the SPLM did not have any knowledge about the existence of these funds. When it was later investigated, the onus landed with Arthur Akuen Chol, who was the SPLM Finance Secretary and Pa'gan Amum, SPLM Secretary General. President Salva Kiir demanded accountability for these funds. It turned out that these funds were given to Dr. John Garang in

Khartoum by President Beshir to start work in southern Sudan. John Garang gave the money to the SPLM Secretary of Finance as the responsible officer since there was no Ministry of Finance yet as Government of southern Sudan was not established.

Pa'gan Amum maintained that he had nothing to do with the money and that it was Arthur Akuen Chol who needed to account for it because he was the Secretary of Finance. Chol was arrested, investigated and jailed, but only to be forcefully released by his community when they broke into prison facility. The Government of southern Sudan did not return him to jail. Chol maintained that he did not misuse funds. He threatened to release names of senior SPLM and Government officials who knew what happened to the funds as he did not want to be scapegoated. Whenever this warning is uttered in southern Sudan, investigations often collapse naturally.

There is a famous saying in South Sudan that, *'Mafi zol biakul barau.'* This roughly translates, 'No one eats alone.' Therefore, those who cook ensure that everyone tastes the soup. The western world was not impressed by the way this case was handled by the government.

Another scandal which involved senior officials was the *'dura saga.'* The Government of southern Sudan came up with a strategy to empower South Sudanese business community by providing them with loans from the Ministry of Finance to purchase and transport dura or maize to the states for food security program.

The project was managed by the then Minister of Finance Kuol Athian. Big contracts were awarded, and full payments were made to local campanies, but most of them were briefcase companies which did not have the capacity to deliver. It was alleged that some state governors signed fake documents of delivery of dura/maize to state governments which never arrived. In return, some of those governors were allegedly given some kickback by owners of the companies. This project was investigated and report after report were produced only to end up on shelves as none of the culprits was made to account. Again, western governments were infuriated by the way this massive case was mishandled. In addition to these two examples, there also appeared the scandal on Letters of Credit (LCs) through the banks and Crisis Management Committee which involved squandering of public funds in which many senior government officials were accused of mismanagement.

The signs of graft were visible from mansions, latest models of vehicles and joint business ventures which were established either in Juba or in foreign capitals. People wondered where our upstarts got resources so quickly to venture on such luxurious lifestyles, given the low salaries of government officials in South Sudan.

Even though the former Government of southern Sudan established an Anti-Corruption Commission which was mandated to investigate these allegations, its findings were never presented in the court of law. This was because the institution was never empowered to persecute those involved in corrupt practices. Instead, it compiled reports and presented them to the Ministry of Legal Affairs and Constitutional Development and after independence, to the Ministry of Justice and Constitutional Affairs for further action on proven cases. That Ministry has the mandate to persecute those involved in criminal activities. However, almost all cases of corruption, but a few, never saw a day in court. Even those that were proven guilty and sentenced to jail terms magically found their way out of prison.

On May 3, 2012, the President wrote letters to 75 senior government officials including sitting and former Ministers and some Governors. The letter appealed to them to return the money embezzled to government accounts which were to be opened for this purpose. The President reported that the amount pilfered at that time in South Sudan was $4.0 billion dollars. The letter stated, 'You can return any amount.' This was an indication that an official didn't have to return the full amount.

The letter was received by his colleagues with great resentment and disappointment. However, some of them were justified in such a reaction. There were some officials who shouldn't have been served with this letter as they were not in the Government of southern Sudan when the mentioned $4.0 billion was squandered. They were Ministers in the national government in Khartoum and there was no way they could have been involved in southern Sudan corruption scandals.

Some Ministers threatened to resign while others promised reciprocation. It took some good will by comrades to calm them down. The President was also worried about mass resignation from the government in a politically charged environment of 2012. He allowed those comrades to continue to persuade their colleagues not to resign as the case was not to be pursued further.

Accordingly, the former government of southern Sudan and later that of independent South Sudan were said to have received $20.0 billion dollars from the oil revenues from 2005 to 2014 (ND shared vision, 2020). The squandered $4.0 billion dollars was said to have been part of this amount (Deng, 2020). However, some analysts along with Dr. Riek Machar refuted that the amount was not entirely accurate as it included some funds that were used for government projects and salaries during the period under consideration. The analysts asked, 'How could you run a government using this amount and at the same time expect the same amount to still be there?' As it is written in any economics book, 'You cannot have your cake and eat it too.'

Reasons and justifications aside for the misuse of 4.0 billion dollars, it is true that massive financial mismagement happened in South Sudan during the time under consideration. Even if the amount may not approximate $4.0 billion dollars, the question on where the money went in South Sudan could not be adequately explained by any official in the government, except to blame mismanagement for it.

In addition to corruption, the western world was also concerned about the apparent lack of democracy in the SPLM which was being fanned by the opposition group within the party. They expressed that President Kiir was not willing to discuss matters of democracy in the basic documents of the SPLM, especially those related to voting, term limits and succession.

During a Juba dinner reception in honour of former Presidents of South Africa and Nigeria, rumour had it that President Salva Kiir told them he was not going to run for President in 2015 (Johnson, 2016). Deng Alor Kuol heard that, and it was also reported that President Salva Kiir informed him about it and that he wanted the SPLM leadership to start dis-cussion on succession. Deng Alor went and informed Pa'gan Amum who was the Secretary General of the SPLM and other senior SPLM officials on this matter. Deng Alor Kuol went on to say that, "The President had shared his decision with his family and told them to prepare for his exit" (Deng, 2020, p.272). Other senior SPLM cadres also corroborated this information.

However, the President maintained that he never told anyone about this and therefore was not happy with those who spread 'unfounded rumors.' This seeming lack of interest in succession planning and preparation for democratic transformation of the rebel movement into a democratic political party put a dent in relations between western powers and the SPLM leadership.

A majority of western powers needed SPLM to open political space for pluralism to flourish in South Sudan. They were concerned about one party dominance in the country as parties formed out of revolutionary movements tend to lean towards singularism and dictatorship. Therefore, they were not entirely against any cleavage if it could peacefully disintegrate the SPLM into manageable political parties which would not dominate political space in South Sudan.

Hence, they encouraged those who worked for its transformation in so long as it would weaken and disintegrate the party in the process. Their intention was clearly demonstrated when the Arusha SPLM reunification process was launched by Chama Cha Mapinduzi (CCM) of Tanzania and African National Congress (ANC) of South Africa. They were against the reunification of the SPLM and therefore dissuaded the two African countries from this engagement calling it 'An endeavor to put a monster's head back to its body, ' to quote one senior leader of those parties who spoke to me on the sidelines of World Political Parties' Conference in Beijing, China in December 2017. Hence, the western countries did not support the reunification of the SPLM morally or financially.

Even relations between the Government of South Sudan and UNMISS were severely damaged when the organization was suspected of interference into the internal affairs of the country. In this regard, President Salva Kiir said, 'That the UN was seeking to take over the country and that the Special Representative of the UN Secretary General in South Sudan was a Co-President.' He said this because there was evidence which indicated that the UN was supporting the opposition forces. For instance, it was reported that UNMISS vehicles were used in the war in 2014 by the SPLM/A-IO forces in Jonglei state. What cemented this allegation even more was the fact that UNMISS never reported that their vehicles were commandeered by the opposition forces. This silence was mis-construed to mean that the organization gave its vehicles to SPLM/A-IO to fight the government.

Furthermore, the Government of South Sudan in March 2014 intercepted 11 UNMISS trucks carrying weapons in Lakes state with waybill marked 'humanitarian goods.' The government used this as another evidence to demonstrate that UNMISS was supplying weapons to the opposition forces. The UNMISS later explained that the weapons were for a Ghanaian battalion of peace-keepers. However, they admitted that they were at fault as they could have transported these weapons by air as stipulated in their protocol for operations.

The failure to fight corruption, dominance of SPLM and alleged lack of democracy exasperated western countries and the international organizations that they fund to the point where they were no longer interested in the system set up in South Sudan. Since they were not able to force President Kiir to dismiss or persecute those accused of corruption in the court of law, the only option was to encourage leadership change in the SPLM which could ultimately result in the change of leadership in the Government of South Sudan.

In addition, some western powers perceived Dr. Riek Machar as an alternative leader in South Sudan. They viewed him as educated, candid and pleasant in disposition. Besides, Dr. Machar always presented himself as a democrat and a change agent. Therefore, their Foreign Ministers; and Ambassadors including those working for the UN system in South Sudan at the time, frequently discussed these issues of change with Dr. Riek Machar, and they quickly got a willing partner. This international dimension of the conflict compounded the internal schisms in the SPLM ending with the tragedy of December 15, 2013.

3.4.4 The Crisis of December 15, 2013

After the death of Dr. John Garang, the SPLM remained a wounded political organization. He was the driving force behind its success during the national liberation struggle and subsequently in the final signature of the Comprehensive Peace Agreement (CPA). The trauma of 21 years of intense fighting and the shock of his death devastated many members of the party to the point of bewilderment and this may possibly explain the undesirable behaviors of some party cadres that appeared later in the country.

The SPLM leadership selection of Salva Kiir as its leader was influenced by two views. First, the SPLM/A is a very hierarchical organization where everyone knows his/her place in the movement as to who comes after whom. In the hierarchy,

Cdr. John Garang was the leader followed by Cdr. Kerbino Kwanyin Bol, Cdr. William Nyuon Bany, Cdr. Arok Thon Arok, Cdr. Salva Kiir Mayardit, etc. Since all the aforementioned founding fathers had passed on, the next person in line was Salva Kiir Mayardit. It was therefore his rightful place to lead the SPLM/A.

The other factor was Dr. Garang's premonition about Salva Kiir in Rumbek, Lakes state, when he presented him to the people that, 'Here is Salva Kiir, he remains with you and he will lead you in southern Sudan' (Johnson, 2016). Many people did not know what Garang meant by this statement. It could have meant that he was going to be busy in Sudan as the First Vice President and that Salva Kiir, his Deputy, was to be running the affairs of southern Sudan on his behalf. However, after his demise, people thought that Garang knew that he was going to die and that he already ordained Salva Kiir as his successor in southern Sudan. That was one of the reasons why the SPLM leadership was unanimous in selecting Salva Kiir without any resistance from potential contenders.

President Salva Kiir performed well as the leader of the movement, especially with regard to the difficult implementation of the CPA, and his ability to buy peace by integrating militia groups into the army and other organized forces in return for their loyalty to South Sudan.

President Salva Kiir, by nature is a gentleman, a good listener, soft spoken, kind-hearted and focused on his objectives. Those qualities distinguish him among many leaders in the SPLM/A. However, his colleagues in the party viewed these qualities as weaknesses and hence, eschewed him as someone who could wear the shoes of Dr. John Garang. Though they initially succumbed to the precept of hierarchy in the movement and the mentioned premonition which propelled Salva Kiir to the helm of the SPLM/A, in retrospect, it is apparent that they regretted their decision.

It was reported in the late 1980s while having dinner with his two top commanders, Kerbino Kwanyin Bol and William Nyuon Bany, that Garang asked the two who they thought would replace him in case something happened to him. It was not an easy question for people so close to that seat and who suspected the intentions of John Garang by asking such question. Both were reported to have deflected the question jokingly saying that nothing was going to happen to their leader to warrant that kind of debate. Dr. John is reportedly said to have mentioned the name of Dr. Riek Machar first as one of his possible successors. This might be the reason why he somehow tried to groom him in the SPLM/A until they fell out in 1991.

Whether Dr. Riek Machar heard that or not, he always saw himself as the rightful successor to Dr. John. He is one of the highly educated leaders in the SPLM/A and government, speaking and writing both English and Arabic fluently. In the words of Nyaba (2016), on any occasion 'Riek Machar filled his position in functions and his presence always overshadowed President Salva Kiir.' The same sentiment is also held by many of Dr. Machar's supporters in the country.

Nevertheless, a majority of senior SPLM cadres do not consider Dr. Machar as the right person for this position due to long held grudges for 1991 SPLM/A split and what they viewed as his leadership deficiencies which were known to whomever worked with him. Therefore, Pa'gan Amum and

Rebecca Nyandeng de Mabior vied for the top post of SPLM in 2013, despite the fact that Dr. Riek Machar was for it, and they were sympathetic to his cause. Even though other cadres like Deng Alor and Dr. Majak d'Agot, did not come out publicly that they wanted to contest, there was a wider public view that they would when the real time for election arrived.

Some senior SPLM cadres challenged their leader Salva Kiir in various ways. First, many people in South Sudan believed that the massive mismanagement of public resources by senior government and party officials was not coincidental. It was considered as a stratagem to unseat the President by making everything intractable in the country to the point where development was botched, thereby making the public angry with the President. Shockingly, people were asking what happened to our liberators? John Gai Yoh (2015) dramatized this point in the 'playing angels' in which the people, leaders, foreign friends and SPLM played being the victim of the other. The problem could not have been lack of skills or education, for the SPLM cadres were well educated and trained in comparison to members of other African revolutionary movements when they got their independence. Any explanation for this kind of behaviour must lie beyond lack of competency and skills.

President Salva Kiir, as his personality dictates did not face his colleagues and discuss the issue of corruption with them to resolve it. There were occasions in his address to the public where he talked about mismanagement and financial corruption in the system. But, he did not want to treat his colleagues in a humiliative manner since he was like a father figure to most of them during the liberation struggle. Besides, he did not want to push them so hard less they rebelled and threaten the future of the referendum on which he had so much riding on.

However, he was clearly let down by his kindness. Instead of kowtowing to President Kiir for cloaking and condoning their behavior, those who held positions in government and SPLM saw this as pusillanimity on his part. Having flexed their political muscles backed by their newly marshalled wealth, they decided to challenge Kiir's leadership both in the SPLM and government.

They used the same malpractices for which they were accused as platform for their political campaign. When President Salva Kiir saw this challenge, he was perturbed and concluded that they had become a threat to his leadership. This forced him to look elsewhere for support even though a majority of the SPLM membership was still supportive of him.

In 2013, the President decided to cast his net wider. A group of former members of the National Congress Party (NCP) of Sudan joined the SPLM *en masse* after South Sudan became independent. These people, some of whom voted for unity with Sudan in the referendum, remained loyal to Khartoum during the liberation struggle. While the President knew that their political loyalty was not for SPLM and South Sudan, he needed their support to neutralize Khartoum's desire to support the opposition against the Government of South Sudan. He was also goaded by his immediate circle to court them as alternatives to the prodigal SPLM cadres.

As soon as contact was made with them, they proved willing and attractive. The National Congress Party of Sudan had a special training for its cadres. They were well disciplined and always respected their leaders. While mingling in the hall of the SPLM House waiting for the SPLM extended Political Bureau meeting to be convened, one former NCP leader said jokingly to senior SPLM cadres whom they consider as recalcitrant that, 'The first principle of leadership is that the leader is always right. The second principle is that even when you find the leader is wrong, the first principle overrides. That means the leader is still right.' He went on. 'If you have to shine the shoes of a leader in order to get what you want, why not?' Those 'NCP principles' utterly contradict the precepts of the majority of cultures of South Sudan which emphasize independence, fairness, egalitarianism and are fiercely against subservience and dictatorship.

That was why Peter Adwok Nyaba, a senior SPLM/A veteran, described these principles held by NCP cadres as 'leader worship, bootlicking and sycophantism which are prone to mislead leaders' (Nyaba, 2017). However, the reality is that many leaders of South Sudan have predisposition to such characters. In no time they became the favourites of J-1.

Immediately, the former NCP cadres were accused of draining the *espirit de corps* of the SPLM party members towards the Chairman of the SPLM President Salva Kiir. It was alleged that they fanned the discord within the SPLM as it was in their best interest to replace those who considered themselves as the autochthons of the party. In the words of Nyaba (2016), 'The NCP operatives in the end elbowed out the SPLM cadres from the favour of their leader.'

There were several attempts by committed SPLM cadres to reconcile the leadership of the party, but those positive gestures ended up in standstill as meetings always turned out to be blaming scene by both sides. It was because of these fissures that the National Liberation Council meetings of the SPLM were postponed several times. President Kiir was frustrated by his colleagues to the point where he had to postpone meetings of the National Liberation Council.

In April 2013, his first action was to withdraw the Presidential powers he delegated to Dr. Riek Machar as Vice President. He also relieved him from chairing the National Reconciliation process as well as dissolved the process itself by decree. This was to serve as a warning that relations between the two men had hit an all-time low.

In May 2013, Dr. Machar sent some of his senior supporters to the United States of America to garner support of the US Government for regime change in South Sudan in favour of the reform agenda under Dr. Machar as an alternative leader in the upcoming 3rd SPLM Convention. The second objective was to seek the support of South Sudanese Diaspora in the US for the same purpose.

The friends of Dr. John Garang and SPLM/A in the USA concurred with their views on regime change and jointly communicated this message to the US Government which seemed to have accepted the idea in principle. To demonstrate their acceptance of the message, the friends of Dr. John Garang and the SPLM/A wrote a letter on June 24, 2013 to President Salva Kiir warning him about the "wrong direction in which the country was headed."

In the letter, they called on the President and the Government of South Sudan to provide basic services to the people; build infrastructure; curb corruption; stop human rights abuses; and the death penalty; just to mention a few. Further and more serioulsly, they stated, 'We cannot turn a blind eye when yesterday's victims become today's perpetrators of crimes.' This letter was a writing on the wall. However, the President and the Government of South Sudan did not accord the letter the seriousness it deserved. They brushed it aside as just another diplomatic blunder by foreign lobbyists; except that these were the same lobbyists who helped us during the liberation struggle.

The second objective of Dr. Riek Machar's team to US was to mobilize the diaspora to reject the Government of President Salva Kiir and accept Dr. Machar as the alternative leader of South Sudan to champion reform in the country. This message was welcomed by some members of Diaspora, the majority of whom were members of the Nuer community.

The President dissolved the National Government on July 23, 2013. All the constitutional post-holders with the exception of the President lost their positions in government. In the same evening, the President suspended SPLM Secretary General Pa'gan Amum and formed a committee to investigate him. He also ordered that Pa'gan Amum must not leave the country until the investigation was completed. The components of the investigation included: (1) accounting for the funds of the party; (2) how he managed the party; and (3) to answer insubordination charges labelled against him.

The Secretary General criticized the party Chairman on SSTV and radio for his suspension and dismissal of then ministers of Finance and Economic Planning, Kosti Manibe and that of Cabinet Affairs, Deng Alor Kuol. The two were investigated by the Anti-Corruption Commission for awarding a contract worth of $8 million dollars to purchase fire safety equipment for government institutions. The contracted company was owned by Gadafi Athorbei.

It was alleged that proper procurement procedures were not followed when the contract was awarded. As a consequence, money was repatriated from Kenya where it was wired to South Sudan with the help of South Sudan Embassy there. Gadafi was arrested, investigated, and sentenced to some years in prison. After serving some time in prison, he was released. The circumstances of his release were not known to the public.

On July 23, 2013, the town of Juba wobbled with rumours of fighting. South Sudan was overwhelmed by unprecedented change in one day. People expected some changes in the government, but not with such magnitude; not literally overnight. People anxiously waited for what the reaction would be from those relieved. Nothing happened that evening, but the calm was prickly as it was too good to be true. People were aware of the conflict and that fighting was only absent temporarily. The question was, 'How long would this built-up pressure hold before exploding?'

Dr. Riek Machar was encouraged by well-wishers to speak to the media to say that there was no problem in the country and that the President had the constitutional mandate to relieve anyone in his government. He did so with Algezira English TV Channel. Many people thought that it was a stunt and did not believe it. It was taken as a political whitewash, but it served its provisional purpose then.

As suspected, the tranquility was short-lived in Juba. The dismissed officials began to harmonize their political strategies to unseat the Chairman in the upcoming 3rd SPLM National Convention. Nonetheless, the discharged officials were not a cohesive entity. Theirs was a combination of groups with many leaders aspiring for the same job. They had to rally behind Dr.

Riek Machar just because he had the Nuer as a fighting force behind him and wanted to use him to get to the top. Dr. Riek Machar was not probably aware of this trick as he could have taken their support with a grain of salt.

In December 2013, several political events took place. In the first week, President Kiir was invited to attend the African Heads of State and Governments Summit organized by then French President Francoise Hollande in Paris. The Summit was to discuss the security situation in Africa, especially the French military intervention in Mali to stop Al-Qaida supported terrorist groups that were poised to overthrow an elected government there.

While the President was away, the SPLM opposition leaders, a majority of whom were in the dissolved government, decided to hold a press conference on Friday, December 6, 2013 at the newly opened SPLM House. The purpose was to voice their dissatisfaction in public with the leadership of the President both in government and the party. It was a palpitating political event in Juba. It was the first of its kind being held by SPLM members against their own Chairman.

Being aware of the behaviour of some of our security personnel, I thought they would attempt to prevent the press conference. This could have opened a Pandora's box to the advantage of the opposition. I made a phone call to then Maj. Gen. Akol Koor Kuc, Director General for Internal Security Bureau, to share with him my thoughts about the press conference and why it should not be prevented. I also advised him that security personnel needed to be on their best behaviour because any assault on the persons of the opposition leaders would turn out to be a disaster for the government and the SPLM.

Then Maj. Gen. Akol Koor assured me that they would not stop the press conference and that he would be there personally to ensure the safety of the opposition leaders. I was thrilled by his response. Those who attended the press conference were predominantly SPLM members who lost their positions during the July reshuffle. Their press statement on Friday December 6, 2013 included the following:

> *The anti-Garang elements inside and outside the SPLM encircled comrade Salva Kiir. There is a shift in decision making process from SPLM national organs to regional and ethnic lobbyists around the SPLM Chairman when it came to appointments to positions in government; that membership of the SPLM and one's participation in the revolutionary struggle became irrelevant. The SPLM Chairman has completely immobilized the party, abandoned collective leadership and jettisoned all democratic pretensions to decision making. The SPLM is no longer the ruling party. The leader of South Sudan Democratic Forum heads the SPLM. We want to bring to the attention of the masses of our people that General Salva Kiir has surrendered the SPLM power to opportunists and foreign agents.*

They demanded that if Chairman Salva Kiir didn't heed their call for an immediate meeting of the National Liberation Council (NLC), they would conduct a public rally on December 14, 2013 to discredit the government. The people of South Sudan didn't take them seriously. This was because they were seen as job seekers who became bitter and angry because they lost their positions. Otherwise, what stopped them from addressing those challenges when they were in senior government and SPLM positions? Besides, who was it that the people of South Sudan blamed for failures of the SPLM and the government? They blamed the leadership of the SPLM as the whole, including them. Therefore, for any of them to ring the bell of anomaly in the party after they were out of government and the party positions was viewed as an exercise in hypocrisy.

When President Kiir returned from Paris on Sunday December 8, 2013, he had to leave for South Africa immediately to attend the funeral of late former South African President Comrade Nelson Mandela. The second deputy Chairman of the SPLM Prof. Dr. James Wani Igga, who was appointed as Vice President of the Republic after the reshuffle, decided to call a counter press conference on Monday December 9, 2013. It was attended by a majority of SPLM members in government and those who did not agree with the agenda of the opposition.

I attended this press conference. During this time, I was just relieved from the position of National Chairperson for Relief and Rehabilitation Commission (RRC) on November 27, 2013 and many people expected me to be with the opposition because it was almost customary for those who lose positions in government to join opposition in South Sudan. My decision stunned friends and political foes alike.

The press conference basically negated that of the opposition. Vice President Prof. Dr. James Wani Igga read the statement which basically accused the group of working to create instability, chaos and disorder in the country. He also accused them of corruption and being the source of developmental lassitude as they squandered financial resources of the country during their tenure from 2005-2013. In short, he recited this age-old adage that, 'Those who live in glasshouses should not throw stones.' It was his way of saying that five fingers were appointing at them as they pointed one finger to the President for the predicaments bedeviling the country.

President Salva Kiir accepted the demand of the opposition and convened the NLC meeting from December 14-15, 2013. The atmosphere of the meeting was tense. The group led by Dr. Riek Machar attended the opening session on 14 December with the exception of Pa'gan Amum who was visibly absent. The reason for his absence was not clear. But we were told that he was confined to his house by security personnel at the orders of the President. Dr. Ann Itto, who was Acting Secretary General of the SPLM, introduced the purpose of the NLC meeting as being a discussion on the SPLM basic documents.

Some people interrupted her saying that she should not start the meeting before prayers were offered. She reminded the people that she was merely laying out the program so that the priests could pray for something they know. When the time came for the then Archbishop Paulino Lukudu Loro of the Catholic Diocese of Juba to speak, he gave a moving speech. He spoke prophetically as though the Holy Spirit showed him what was about to take place. He warned:

> *I see that you are not happy in this meeting. I want you to know that this is Christmas season and people need to celebrate this holiday in peace. I would like to ask you to postpone this meeting because I think it will generate crisis and violence. You know we came out of war, and we don't want war anymore. Our people are tired of war.*

After this emotional speech with his usual trembling voice, he called up on then Archbishop Primate Dr. Daniel Deng Bul of the Episcopal Church of the Sudan and South Sudan to join him as they both offered prayer for peace. The Muslim cleric, after a serious admonition for the leadership of the SPLM, also followed the same line of prayer for peaceful dialogue in the SPLM. H.E. Hilde Johnson, Special Representative of the UN Secretary General and Head of UNMISS appealed for peace and reconciliation in the meeting to be the top priority.

Many people always like to talk in SPLM meetings, but not in this one. It was time for the President of the Republic and Chairman of the SPLM to take to the podium. The room was dead silent. One could almost hear a pin drop in a room packed with people. It felt like conflict was imminent.

One of the earlier indications of the problem was that when President Kiir entered the hall, everyone was already seated. He greeted his Second Deputy in the party Dr. James Wani Igga, but not Dr. Riek Machar, his First Deputy, who was seated immediately next to him. This was clear enough to indicate the imminence of crisis at least for those who were not privy to the internal squabbles of the SPLM.

There were three issues which stood out in Chairman Kiir's speech. First, he accused the group led by Dr. Riek Machar of insubordination when in their December 6 press conference, they gave him the ultimatum that if he did not call for NLC meeting, they would go for a public rally. Second, he emphasized that he would never allow the episode of 1991 to repeat itself. This became the most ambiguous and interpreted sentence of his leadership by many analysts. Did he mean that he would not allow the SPLM to divide again? Or did he mean that should there be a split, something like Bor massacre would not occur? Or did he mean that it would not be the Dinka to be murdered? No one knew what he meant by such a statement. Third, the Chairman listed his credentials within the SPLM as a liberator who never betrayed the cause of the people. He clearly directed his second and third statements at Dr. Riek Machar.

I watched Dr. Riek Machar's body language as President Salva Kiir was speaking. He sat with his head turned to where we were seated. His fingers were crisscrossed and held his chin with his two thumbs. He was avoiding eye contact with Salva Kiir at the podium. His eyes were flickering with anger. Everyone in the room knew that Dr. Machar was very uncomfortable.

Then, Aguil Machut, who was a member of the NLC for SPLM Australia Chapter, stood up in the meeting and started to sing a revolutionary SPLA song in Dinka. Usually when someone starts a revolutionary song, those in attendance would join in the singing, but not on this day. She sang alone thereby literally interrupting President Salva Kiir from his speech. Since she kept singing and Salva Kiir stood there to let her sing and no one joined, he decided to sing along with her.

In fact, Aguil was known for starting songs in any SPLM function; therefore, there was nothing particular about this occasion which would put her motives in question. However, many people who speak Dinka thought that the content of the song was not appropriate in that conflict charged environment.

After the speech of the Chairman of the SPLM, it was declared that all members of the NLC would return to the meeting in the afternoon to debate the basic documents of the party. The rest of us were now excused from the meeting.

Indeed, NLC members returned to the meeting in the afternoon including Dr. Riek Machar, Taban Deng Gai, Rebecca Nyadeng de Mabior, just to mention a few from the opposition. Many of the articles in the constitution were passed without any problem as the two groups did not have any concerns about them.

Concerns arose with articles dealing with the method of voting and 5% seats allocated to minority ethnic groups. Dr. Riek Machar raised issue with the proposed voting mechanism in the party. In the text, the document read that, 'All voting in the SPLM meetings shall be conducted by show of hands.' This was taken directly from the 2008 SPLM Constitution. The group of Dr. Riek Machar had issue with this because he believed that people would be intimidated if they voted by show of hands. His argument was in line with the internationally accepted practice. However, his real motive to insist on secret ballots was such that those who pretended to be supporters of President Salva Kiir would vote for him without being noticed by the Chairman of the SPLM. Therefore, he preferred voting by secret ballot.

Salva Kiir and his supporters rejected this proposition and contended that voting needed to be by show of hands. Their reason was that some members of the SPLM couldn't read or write. Therefore, they could not fill ballot papers without being assisted by someone else. This meant that those they voted for would be known by whoever assisted them. If this was the case then, why waste time on a secret ballot? This argument made sense on the surface, but it was also a maneuver to ensure that no one from his supporters would defect to Dr. Machar. When this issue of 'voting mechanism' was put to the test by a show of hands on the floor of the NLC, Dr. Riek Machar's group only got 8 votes out of 128 members present. It was a chastening defeat for Dr. Machar and his group.

Then Taban Deng Gai took issue with 5% minority quota which the draft constitution stipulated that the Chairperson would appoint. He argued that those 5% would become loyalist to whoever appointed them and therefore would vote for him/her in the Convention. He insisted that this quota must be deleted from the document. He maintained that all positions must be subjected to free and fair competition and that there was no need for a special quota.

He was asked to suggest how minorities would be represented given the fact that they could not compete with larger ethnic groups and win seats. His alternative method for minority representation did not convince many members of the NLC. As a result, it suffered a similar defeat by 8 to 128 votes in the meeting. This loss was a disaster to the internal SPLM opposition in Juba. Since the group of Dr. Riek Machar seemed to champion the cause for democracy, one thought that this was the end of the standoff. On the contrary, it was just the beginning of it.

In the next meeting on Sunday afternoon, Dr. Machar and his group boycotted the meeting and he spoke to a Sudan Tribune journalist who reported the reasons why on December 15, 2015, the day the group of Dr. Machar did not show up for the meeting:

> *Machar and his colleagues attended the first day of the NLC meeting on Saturday, where they participated in deliberations on the passing of the basic documents, namely the manifesto and the constitution. However, the party*

Deputy Chairman said Kiir's statements during the meeting had deviated from the spirit of dialogue and rec- onciliation which had been called for by SPLM supporters. He said the Chairman, who has previously been accused of dictatorial tendencies, did not heed to the voice of wisdom by Bishops and Sheikhs who graced the opening session to remind the leaders on the need for dialogue and reconcilia- tion. Kiir's statements were of hostility, [and provided] no room for political dialogue. He said his group has decided to dissociate itself from this undemocratic process amid fears it would pass undemocratic resolutions in the meeting. Machar added that his group did not want to be involved in the dismissal process of the party's suspended Secretary General, Pa'gan Amum, whom he said was tried in absentia by a hand-picked committee appointed by Kiir.

With this defeat of the opposition, the political barometer in Juba rose. It was clear that there was no way the group of Dr. Riek Machar would get what they wanted as democracy failed them on the floor of the NLC meeting. This reminded me of my discussion with him in his office on May 6, 2013 when I said to him that he should not start a campaign early as this would make it difficult to prepare the SPLM documents because each of them would want the documents to be reflec- tive of their individual interests.

However, he never saw this coming. Now, Dr. Riek Machar and his group were in a panic mode. They had to boycott the second day of the meeting as shown in his words above. In the afternoon of December 15, 2013, when the NLC members returned to the hall for the meeting, they found that Dr. Machar wrote a note that his group could not attend the meeting any longer because the atmosphere in the meeting was hostile as he had described it to the Sudan Tribune journalist above.

Instead of questioning the motive for the group's decision to stay away from the meeting, some members of NLC were thrilled that they now would do their work without any irritation from the opposition. In accordance with the procedures, more than a quorum was present and the meeting could not be postponed because a few members decided to boycott it.

At about 7:00pm on the same day, I went to greet Gen. James Hoth Mai, then SPLA Chief of General Staff, who just returned from visiting his family in Australia and transited via Addis-Ababa to attend the ceremony of his master's degree graduation. When I came near his house, I found that there were many vehicles and bodyguards at the vicinity. I assumed that some Generals were with him. Indeed, when I entered his sitting room upstairs, I found many Generals from almost all the organized forces.

From the looks of things, I realized that something was afoot. I greeted them and said to James Hoth Mai that I would wait for him down-stairs. He responded that they were at the conclusion of their meeting. Indeed, they finished very quickly, and James Hoth Mai accompanied them to their vehicles. I also joined them as they walked to their cars. I particularly noticed the body language of Gen. Pieng Deng Kuol, who was Inspector General of South Sudan Police, and I asked him if he was okay. I asked him because he looked deflated and wore plain cloth with a shirt whose collar was not folded on one side. However, looks could be deceiving. He responded in the affirmative.

When I returned to the house with Gen. James, I asked him what the matter was about. For those who know him, James

Hoth Mai, never talks much to people about security issues. He only said to me that the Generals went to report to him some challenges which they needed to address. I said, 'But Pieng Deng didn't really look well.' He replied without elaboration, '*Ay, indu machakil.*' Meaning, 'Yes, he has problems.' I told him that I came to greet him and that I was proceeding to my home.

As I was walking to my vehicle, one of the supporters of Dr. Machar who was in the house of Gen. James followed and asked me what I discussed with James. I told him that there was nothing more than to welcome him back to Juba from Australia. Then he uttered to me these words which I remember to this day, 'Will something we have planned for so many months really fail today?' I responded, 'Well, this is the nature of democracy you are calling for. I believe that you just need another strategy to get your feet on the ground again.' Poor me! I missed his point completely. I thought he was talking about his group's defeat at the NLC meeting in the afternoon when all articles were passed to their disappointment. No, he had just told me what was about to happen. I only realized what he meant after what followed at 10:30pm on that fateful night of December 15, 2013.

3.4.5 December 15, 2013:
The Emergence of the Coup and Elimination Theories

No one could tell with certainty what happened that night because either side had a different story to tell. And even within the same groups, there were different versions. The only known thing was that December 15, 2013 was a dreadful and tragic night for South Sudan. It was on this night that what Nyaba (2016) described as the animal in the people of South Sudan woke up.

The answer to what happened that night was polarized. Based on who and the ethnicity of the person, one would almost certainly guess the answer. A majority of the Nuer said that the tragedy was started by elected President Salva Kiir Mayardit and his own ethnic group, the Dinka, led by the Jieng Council of Elders (JCE) to eliminate Dr. Riek Machar and the opposition group members so that Dinka leadership in South Sudan would continue without any hindrance. On the other hand, a majority of Dinka said that the crisis was started by Dr. Riek Machar and the Nuer ethnic group to usurp the leadership of the country by force of arms from President Kiir.

As is well known, these two views were provincial because the genesis of the crisis was not based on ethnicity. It was caused by a power struggle within the SPLM leadership as to who should lead the SPLM and become the flag bearer of the party in the general elections scheduled for June 2015. If the conflict was ethnic based, how would one explain why some Dinka supported Dr. Riek Machar and majority of Nuer leadership and intellectuals supported President Salva Kiir? It is known that the cause of the conflict was a power struggle within the party, but the war was fought predominantly along ethnic lines making it almost impossible for many analysts to recognize the cause from the consequence.

However, it is important to explain what went wrong from the perspectives of the belligerents first before delving into further analysis. The first theory to explain the cause of war was advanced by Dr. Machar and his supporters that President Kiir and his associates planned to eliminate the opposition leaders who were viewed as his potential successors in the SPLM. In order to get rid of them, a story was concocted that Dr. Riek Machar, and his associates, staged a *coup d'état* against the Government of President Kiir.

Fearing the fact that the SPLA was dominated by the Nuer ethnic group, Salva Kiir, Paul Malong Awan (then Governor of Northern Bahr El Ghazal), who later became Chief of General Staff of the SPLA in April 2014, and other senior military and political figures from Bahr El Ghazal states, embarked on training a private army outside of the SPLA establishment to protect their regime. They said that it was this private army which massacred the Nuer in Juba from December 16-20, 2013.

According to the opposition, this private army was trained and graduated in 2013 in Luri, the presidential ranch. In fact, there was a graduation ceremony witnessed on SSTV of troops in Luri in which the President addressed the soldiers in Dinka language and the then SPLA Chief of Staff, Gen. James Hoth Mai was not in attendance.

It was speculated that Gen. James Hoth Mai refused to attend the graduation of this group because of his disapproval of the utilization of a private army. According to Nyaba (2016), 'these 15,000 troops, with units popularly known as Gelweng, Dotkubany and Mathiang Anyor, were recruited from Warrap and Northern Bahr El Ghazal states.' Pinaud (2021, p. 136), further observed that "They were the ones used to carry out the Nuer massacre in Juba from December 16-20, 2013." Edwards (2016) also corroborated and expressed the same sentiments although with scathing details. According to this view, Dr. Riek Machar and the opposition group were mere victims of a conspiracy to eliminate them so that President Kiir could continue to rule the country without any challenge.

As it is, this theory seems to explain all that happened, but falls short in explaining a number of issues. It is obvious that there was power struggle among the two groups in the SPLM and this was the real cause of the crisis in the country. If one side had the means to wrestle the other to the ground, it would have done so without hesitation. This analysis begins with the issue of a private army which needs clarification.

First, the SPLA general headquarters sent out a call to all the ten states to each contribute 5000 new recruits to join the army because of the fighting in Heglig (Panthou) in April 2012 with the Sudan. The only states which responded positively to this call for recruitment were Upper Nile, Unity, Warrap and Northern Bahr El Ghazal, probably because they border the Sudan and were most of the times at the receiving end of the wrath of the Sudanese Government.

The rest of the states did not bring any recruits because no volunteers reported themselves. However, the fighting in Heglig did not continue and therefore the SPLA headquarters cancelled the recruitment call. They took some 600 recruits from Upper Nile and added them to Division One (Jamus) because the commander there had equipment for a such number. They disbanded the rest of the recruits.

Warrap and Northern Bahr El Ghazal states recruited 15, 000 to this national call. When it was cancelled, Governors Paul Malong Awan and Nyandeng Malek de Liech did not want to disband them. They convinced the leadership that they would maintain them if the SPLA general headquarters had no capacity to feed them. They kept the recruits in Pantit Training Center despite the directive of the SPLA command to disband the group. This was where the bone of contention and suspicion commenced between the SPLA and the two governors of those states.

It was alleged by many analysts that the reason why the governors of these two states kept their recruits was because they did not trust the SPLA. The SPLA was dominated by the Nuer ethnic group and commanded by a Nuer Chief of General Staff to protect the President who was a Dinka. Governor Paul Malong Awan was known for stating that the Nuer were going to take power from President Kiir since they dominated the army and Dr. Riek Machar could challenge the President any time. This could be the possible explanation as to why the two governors refused to disband these recruits after the directive from the SPLA Chief of General Staff to do so.

The composition of the Presidential Guards' Unit is one Brigade (3000 soldiers). Although there was a plan by the SPLA general headquarters to upgrade this Brigade to Divisional level, it did not materialize. It was sometime in 2013, the Command of the Presidential Guards' Unit (Tiger) decided to add 330 soldiers from Pantit Training Center, and they were brought to Luri with full knowledge of SPLA general headquarters. These were the ones that President Kiir addressed in Dinka language in his ranch at Luri which was broadcasted on SSTV. There was a question as to why the Chief of General Staff of the SPLA did not attend this ceremony. According to security and military analysts, that was not mandatory, but there was also no harm if he was there or vice versa.

These new recruits were added to the existing Brigade, and this brought their total number to 3, 330. The SPLA general headquarters pays their salaries although it does not have structural command over them in accordance with their institutional set up. Therefore, the Presidential Guards Unit is part of the SPLA and cannot be misconstrued as a private force.

The remaining 14, 670 that were left in Pantit Training Center, Northern Bahr El Ghazal state, were never utilized until after the crisis started in December 2013. During the crisis, a majority of the Nuer elements in the SPLA defected and joined Riek Machar. Because of that, there was a need to reinforce the SPLA. Since they were trained and ready for deployment, it was only logical for the SPLA headquarters to utilize them.

Based on the evidence gathered from security sources, it was stated that these soldiers did not come to Juba during the days of the 'Nuer Massacre' from December 16-20, 2013. The only time they came through Juba was when they were deployed to fight in Bor and Malakal and that was on 23 December after Juba incident. This means that the Nuer massacre in Juba was not likely carried out by them since they were not physically here. The Gelweng, Dotkubany, Mathiang Anyor, Petroleum Protection Force and Abuchiok were Dinka civilian militias who fought alongside government forces mimicking the role of the Nuer white army[5] alongside the opposition forces. Therefore, there is nothing peculiar to say about their role in the war.

The Government of South Sudan advanced the 'Coup theory' when on the evening of December 16, 2013, in the heart of the conflict, the President came on the national SSTV and pronounced that the SPLA and other organized forces had quelled a coup staged by Dr. Riek Machar and his associates. This was the first time the country put a name to the fighting in Juba.

I talked to myself and asked, 'Is this a coup?' My first natural reaction was to call a couple of Generals in the SPLA to ask if we had just thwarted a coup. The response depended on who I called. Some said it was a coup while others said it was a mutiny. The evidence of the coup centered on December 6, 2013 press conference conducted by the leaders of the opposition in the SPLM House in Juba. This was also coupled with the mobilization of Nuer officers and soldiers in the SPLA, and other organized forces as well as the white army in the villages to fight the Government of President Kiir by the opposition leadership and their supporters.

There was astonishment nationally, regionally and internationally about the coup pronouncement. The next day, Dr. Riek Machar spoke on international media, especially the BBC and

---

5 White army refers to organized civilian Nuer youth formed to fight and defend Nuer interests militarily from both internal and external foes. The expression is so used to distinguish them as non-uniformed civilian fighters from uniformed organized forces. The real distinction between the white army and the organized forces is from what they wear rather than what they do.

Al Gezira networks that he ran away for his life from Juba and that he did not stage any coup. The world was confused as to what was truthful: a coup against President Kiir or an attempt to eliminate the opposition.

The world did not agree with the coup theory because there were no Generals in the SPLA or other organized forces linked to it and the government agencies which arrested the alleged coup plotters did not present strong evidence to defend their case in the court. The arrest of the Group of ten politicians, popularly known as G-10 or Former Detainees (FDs) was simply viewed as an action based on personal vendettas by 'Salva Boys' who were now firmly in control of the Office of the President, against 'Garang Boys.'

The two theories or perspectives are deficient to explain what happened. As submitted in the previous sections, the fact that war was inevitable in South Sudan was not a surprise to those in leadership positions in the country. What could not have been deciphered was when, how, where and who would start it. From the initial stages, Dr. Riek Machar was not interested in bringing about reforms in the SPLM using military means. He was clear on this position in the media and to his associates.

However, when the entire government was dissolved on July 23, 2013, he got a lot of followers from the deposed senior SPLM leaders. He felt he had a formidable group to work with. In fact, with him were historical SPLM/A cadres: Pa'gan Amum, Deng Alor, Madut Biar, Kosti Manibe, John Luk Jock, Dr. Majak Agot, Rebecca Nyandeng de Mabior, Gen. Oyay Deng Ajak, Gen. Gier Chuang Aluong, Dr. Peter Adwok Nyaba, Taban Deng Gai, and many others who later on retracted from the group on the D-Day of December 6, 2013 for personal and regional considerations.

Dr. Riek Machar was emboldened by the presence of SPLM heavy weights on his side for the first time since the days of 1991. However, he did not know that they were not there for him. They were there for their agenda. They only wanted to use him as a Trojan horse to get what they wanted since he had the backing of the majority of Nuer who often never seem to question his motives.

Around August 2013 after the reshuffle, the opposition engaged in a massive mobilization of Nuer officers in the organized forces, the white army, and the chiefs in the villages. They told them that the Dinka removed Dr. Riek Machar and gave the position of Vice President to an Equatorian. They said that the Dinka were determined to prevent any Nuer from becoming President of South Sudan. Most of the Nuer believed that after Salva Kiir, it must be a Nuer to take the position of President.

The fact that the position of Vice President went to Equatoria was a subtle indication that a Nuer might not actually be President after Salva Kiir. Since this was not an analytical group, the situation ignited rage in them. The method they knew best was to fight to get what they wanted.

On December 15, 2013, it became clear that reforms would not be achieved through democratic means since Riek Machar's reform agenda was defeated on the floor of the NLC meeting. He threw in the towel and those opposition leaders who thought of using the military means to force President Kiir out of power were now left to do their magic. In fact, there were a handful of them and those were predominantly from the Nuer community with leaders from other ethnic groups providing moral and financial muscle to the operation.

In fact, one Director General (DG) of the National Security Bureau reported that he caught one leader of the opposition in flagrante delicto distributing money to soldiers for this operation. When he asked that leader why he was doing that to destroy the country, he replied 'hakuma bitakumda, hindu saa'tein bas, wa yega.' Meaning, your government has two hours only and it will fall. When I asked this DG why he didn't arrest the man, he said 'No one believed what we were saying Peter Lam until the first bullet was actually fired. Then the people and the system panicked.'

On that same day, one senior Nuer person in the group of Dr. Riek Machar directed a Nuer Lt. Colonel in Gyiada (Presidential guards' headquarters) to start fighting or else the Dinka were planning to disarm and arrest them that evening. It was this Nuer officer who fired the first bullet and killed his deputy (a Dinka) who was on duty that night. Then the body-guards joined in the shooting. This was what ignited the fight among the Presidential guards at about 10:30pm on December 15, 2013 in Giyada headquarters.

This account was also corroborated by other sources. In the report of the AU Commission of Inquiry on South Sudan (AUCISS, 2014), almost all the senior South Sudan security and military officers interviewed pointed fingers at this partic-ular Nuer Lt. Colonel, as the starter of the fight confirming the very point that was made earlier.

In March 2014, the same officer also boasted, on the streets of Addis-Ababa, to Nuer supporters of Dr. Riek Machar about how he started the war in Juba. It was a source of pride for him to talk about. I and my colleagues were in Addis-Ababa at that time and his revelation made him a hero in the eyes of the Nuer community there.

However, certain individuals presented a different account of how the war started and this was the account of many in the opposition. They believed that war started when Maj. General Marial Chinoung, the Commander of the Republican guards or Tiger Brigade, ordered the Nuer soldiers in the Presidential guards' unit to be disarmed (Nyaba, 2016; Pinaud, 2021). Then the Nuer refused to be disarmed and in the process, the fight started. The same individuals also stated that the President brought Ugandan forces to Juba on December 13, 2013, exactly two days before the incident suggesting that there was a plan for war in which Uganda would be involved.

As far as facts are concerned, there is something to be said about this presentation of events. Ugandan forces came to Juba on December 18, 2013. I witnessed the coming of Ugandan helicopters to Juba in the afternoon of December 18. This was also confirmed by a UNMISS report (2014) that Ugandan forces came to Juba on December 18, 2013. To suggest that Ugandan forces were in Juba prior to December 18, 2013 was to misrepresent the facts.

As for the disarmament of the Nuer elements in the Presidential guards' unit, it is necessary for numbers to do the talking for they don't lie. First, Presidential guards were pre-dominantly composed of former bodyguards of Gen. Salva Kiir, Gen. Paulino Matip Nhial and Gen. Dr. Riek Machar. General Matip was the Deputy Commander-in-Chief of the SPLA until his natural death in 2013. The bodyguards of President Kiir were predominantly Dinka, those of Dr. Machar were predominantly Nuer and those of Paulino Matip were exclusively Nuer from Unity state. The total number of Presidential Guards was 3000 as presented earlier. They were increased with 330 from Pantit, Northern Bahr El Ghazal state and that brought their total to 3, 330 in December 2013.

From the total Presidential Guards, 1, 800 of them were exclusively from Nuer community and 1, 530 were predominantly Dinka with other ethnic groups marginally represented. Now assume that all the guards were actively on duty that night, (which was not the case) how could 1, 530 disarm 1, 800 Nuer soldiers? That was a very unlikely scenario, if not, impossible. The Nuer intellectuals with this knowledge know that there is something wrong with the Nuer disarmament claim as a cause of war because it was implausible. Moreover, what kind of disarmament would be conducted at night? Where would Maj. Gen. Marial find all the 1800 Nuer to be disarmed in that night when they were not all on duty?

Secondly, Maj. Gen. Marial Chinoung, who was accused of disarming the Nuer elements in the Presidential guards' unit, said to SSTV that he was asleep in his house when the first bullet was fired. Earlier in the day, Marial and his command resolved a problem which was stirred up by the same Nuer Lt. Colonel who claimed that he was told the Nuer in the Presidential guards would not receive their salary. Marial told him that all the salaries would be paid the next day. That seemed to have calmed down the situation. Therefore, when Marial Chinoung went to his home, he did not know that it was not about the payment of salaries. It was a search for a cause to start fighting as the pressure was mounting on the Nuer Lt. Colonel by the senior supporters of Dr. Riek Machar.

Dr. Machar and his close associates escaped from Juba as soon as the first bullet was fired on the night of December 15, 2013. It was reported that he waited near Terekeka to see how events would unfold in Juba town. Clearly, there was no command structure among the Nuer troops because when they captured the Tiger headquarters that evening, they could have marched to J-1 Presidential Palace. However, they did not because their coordinators fled, and orders and leadership were not being given. They became confused as to what to do next. The Nuer Lt. Colonel who started the fight ran together with Dr. Riek Machar and his close associates in the same evening.

Furthermore, the coordinators of these soldiers, who were mainly opposition politicians, relied heavily on junior officers to do the work for them which negatively affected the outcome of their plan. This disorganization within the rank and file of the opposition army and politicians led to the existence of the 'coup' to be denied by its orchestrators. In other words, the coup was too disorganized to be recognized by international political and military analysts. But, why did Dr. Riek Machar, his close associates and the man who fired the first bullet run away together that evening if they did not have any connection with the fight in the Tiger headquarters? The answer is anyone's guess.

CHAPTER FOUR

Responses of Various Stakeholders to the Crisis of December 15, 2013

As the country was shocked by the events of December 15, 2013, various stakeholders responded in varying degrees as shown below.

4.1. The Response of Certain Dinka Elements in the Organized Forces to the Crisis of December 15, 2013

In the morning of December 16, 2013, Bilpam Military headquarters was attacked by the rebels at about 4:00am. The fighting lasted until about 11:00am when the opposition forces were dislodged. It was after the end of this fighting that the Nuer in the vicinities of 107, Mangateen, New Site and Eden City were targeted by certain Dinka elements in the SPLA and other organized forces under the pretext that they were searching for armed opposition fighters who had hid themselves in the houses. This quickly turned into a hunt for Nuer people in which men, women and children were exterminated in big numbers.

I was alerted to this fact when Nuer men, women and children ran to seek protection in my house located in the community of Mangateen. I had a few bodyguards at home and people thought that my house was safe. I didn't believe this until the children of John Jal, a Nuer MP from Jonglei state Assembly, ran to my house and said that their father and his brother-in-law were shot in front of them. Immediately, more Nuer people filled the roads of my neighbourhood in an attempt to seek protection. Their story was that the Nuer were being killed in their homes. I realized the situation was getting out of hand. It was no longer about the government and the opposition fighting. Nuer civilians were being targeted and this was the consequence rather than the cause of war as many in the opposition portrayed it.

I was one of the first people to call Gen. James Hoth Mai, then SPLA Chief of General Staff, to tell him that Nuer civilians were being hunted and killed in their homes. He was astounded! It felt like it was the first time he heard about this. He asked me, 'How could this happen? Have you seen people being killed?' I responded in the affirmative. Little did he know that his telephone lines would be inundated with similar calls from various corners of the city. When he sent out troops to stop the carnage, the killers would fire on them and fighting ensued. That became the new normal for operations in Juba from December 16-20, 2013.

Almost all the quarters in Juba where the Nuer lived were targeted for killing. According to various agencies' reports, this house-to-house hunting of the Nuer covered the communities of 107, Mangateen, Eden City, New Site, Khor Uliang, Gurey, Nyakuron, Customs, Gudeles, and others (HRW, 2014; UNMISS, 2014; Pinaud, 2021). The Nuer who didn't live in the Nuer concentrated neighbourhoods were also targeted as their homes were shown to assailants by some of their neighbours.

Nuer elements who remained in government service in various locations across the country were also targeted by their Dinka colleagues. For example, some Nuer military commanders and government officials who didn't rebel were attacked at night in their homes and units in the organized forces in Juba, parts of Upper Nile, Jonglei, Greater Bahr El Ghazal and Equatoria states. This forced them to run either to UNMISS POC sites to seek protection or to the bush where they ended up with Dr. Riek Machar.

A case example was former Minister for Wildlife Conservation and Tourism Changson Lew Chang, who was attacked in his house by gunmen. His nephew was killed in the attack. Though Changson stayed in the house of Gen. James Hoth Mai for a while, he did not feel safe. He had to go to UNMISS POC site for protection until he decided to join Riek Machar in the bush.

Similar assaults were also launched in Juba against the homes of Gen. Simon Gatwech Dual, Gen. James Maluit, Brig. Gen. Henry Lam Juch and so forth. If General Simon Gatwech Dual was not attacked in his house in Juba, he probably would not have ended up with Dr. Riek Machar and became his army's Chief of Staff.

Even then Brigadier Gen. Peter Gatwech Gai, Commander

of the SPLA Commandos, who captured Bor town from Nuer rebels in January 2014, was attacked in his office in Giyada in March 2014. He was rescued with a bullet-proof vehicle availed by his colleagues. According to eye- witnesses, 85 soldiers were killed in this attack even though South Sudan Human Rights Commission (SSHRC, 2015) reported only 35 soldiers and six civilians as dead.

Certain individuals from Dinka community also formed militia groups in Juba who also carried out attacks against the Nuer. Some of them were disarmed and arrested by the SPLA along with many other elements who were involved in the massacre from December 16-20, 2013. However, they escaped from detention centers apparently assisted by some senior relatives in the government. According to Johnson (2016), the Ministry of Defense and other military sources confirmed the detention of many suspects of the December massacre, but none of them were tried in the court of law.

There were many ill-conceived reasons for targeting the Nuer in the City of Juba. First, there were certain people who believed that all the Nuer were supporters of Dr. Riek Machar who was accused of staging a coup against President Salva Kiir Mayardit. Their strategy was to purge the town from coup plotters. Second, there were also other individuals who carried out revenge killing against the Nuer for alleged killings of their relatives in the past military operations including that of Bor massacre in 1991(Edwards, 2016). And finally, such tactics were also employed by those who wanted to occupy positions of their Nuer colleagues in various units of govern-ment. The idea was to kill or chase them away so that vacancies were created to be filled by them. As it turned out, the killing of Nuer people in Juba backfired as those who were chased away ended up with Dr. Riek Machar. In other words, the killing of the Nuer did the recruitment for Dr. Riek Machar and deprived President Salva Kiir of substantive support from the greater Nuer community.

The opposition (Lok, 2016), United Nations (2014) and Pinaud (2021) estimated that about 20,000 Nuer people were killed from December 16-20, 2013 in Juba. Although that number is in the higher end and could not be verified or cor-roborated in the field in Juba, the psychological weight of the tragedy was more than a number. Based on our local assessment in Juba, we believe that at least a couple of thousands lost their lives, including those who died in the battle field. Each Nuer district knows how many they lost during the massacre. There was no need to guess the number of the deceased when an accurate figure could be found.

There was no evidence of any government policy to exter-minate the Nuer as the opposition claimed. What is plausible is that certain individuals from Dinka within the organized forces decided to take laws into their own hands by murdering and targeting Nuer people in Juba. Even though investigation reports by Edwards, (2016), AU (AUCISS, 2014), HRW (2014; 2016), Pinaud (2021) and UNMISS (2014) suggested that there existed an informal coordinating structure which ordered the murder of the Nuer in the four quadrants of the city, they inadvertently validate the point made earlier that there was no formal structure or government policy to this effect.

The majority of the Nuer leadership in government did not agree with Dr. Machar in his quest to snatch political power from an elected President because there was no justification for it. They believed that he was going to be the next President if he had the virtue of patience. Allegations of domination or alienation of the Nuer from participation in government as the possible cause of conflict between the two leaders is not supported by available evidence, as the Nuer occupied some of the highest government offices in the country, especially in the governments before July 23, 2013.

Dr. Machar's only fortune came with the unfortunate reaction of certain Dinka elements in the army and other organized forces against the Nuer civilians. If the Nuer were not targeted in Juba, war could have ended in a very short time. It was only when the Nuer were murdered, that their relatives were enraged, and revenge became the driver of the conflict masking the political objectives on which it was anchored.

Dr. Riek Machar and his supporters held tight on the 'Nuer massacre' as the only *rai·son d'ê·tre* of the conflict thereby concealing their role as the source of the crisis in the country. They were viewed by the Nuer all over the world as defenders of their rights.

The voice of the Nuer leaders who remained in the Government of South Sudan was neither heard by the government nor by the Nuer opposition. Most of the Nuer people closed their minds as they were told by Dr. Machar and his supporters that all the Nuer were exterminated in Juba. In the minds of Nuer people in the villages, memories of 1991 were fresh. According to a report by Amnesty International (1995), more than 72 Nuer SPLA officers and large numbers of Nuer soldiers, who were stationed in Equatoria and Bahr El Ghazal Regions as well as other Dinka areas in Upper Nile Region, were murdered in cold blood after Dr. Machar's *coup d'état* against Dr. John Garang in Nasir in 1991.Therefore, there was a reason to believe that what Dr. Riek Machar and his associates told them about the total annihilation of the Nuer in Juba was sacrosanct.

When Nuer leaders in government tried to convince their people in the villages not to fight their Dinka neighbours, it was almost an impossible task as bad news already reached the villages.The response of many relatives was that 'All our people are murdered in Juba, why are you pretending to be Nuer?' They thought the people speaking to them from Juba in Nuer language were imposters. One of my relatives in the village told me, "You are a Dinka who killed my brother Peter Lam Both and you are using his phone. Please don't call me again. If I were near you, I would kill you right now." No matter how hard I tried to convince him that it was me, he couldn't believe it.This shows how dangerous the information that went to the Nuer communities across the world was.

4.2. The Response of Certain Nuer Elements in the Organized Forces and the White Army to the Crisis of December 15, 2013

If the Nuer were not murdered, it was believed that Dr. Riek Machar could have fled alone with his close associates.The rest of it could have been history. But Dr. Riek Machar is always a fortunate human being. Situations which he has not worked for always turn out in his favour.The reaction of certain Dinka elements made him survive politically and become a hero to the Nuer people. He used the Nuer massacre as a card to gain political support from this community worldwide. Not only that, Dr. Machar gained political support from many countries and human rights organizations across the world because of the massacre. The news of the Nuer massacre in Juba was reported by major international media houses.

The majority of the Nuer in Juba also phoned their family members in Jonglei, Unity, Upper Nile states as well as the Diaspora describing to them the gruesome carnage inflicted on them. The rage of family members in the villages was beyond control. I personally received several phone calls from my county and other counties across South Sudan as well as the Diaspora. Some called to know if the news of the massacre was true, while others did so to confirm if I was still alive. The latter was easier to answer than the former. How could one answer such a question without generating more incitement for revenge? The answer had to be diligently worded…that is to confirm in ways that would not alarm and generate any action of reprisal. I had also lost family members and friends alike in Juba. It was very difficult to remain cool headed in a crazy environment of carnage.

The incident which started as a power struggle within the SPLM now turned out to be a national crisis with an ethnic dimension. For a majority of the Nuer, it was no longer about a political position for Dr. Riek Machar. It was about revenge for the Nuer that were massacred in Juba. Dr. Riek Machar exploited this and utilized it as though it were his popularity among the Nuer which generated such reaction. In confirmation to this, he told the international media during the fighting in December 2013 that the 'white army' was under his firm command (Johnson, 2016).

As the war continued to rage in Juba and its vicinity on

December 16-17, 2013, Maj. Gen. Peter Gatdeet Yak, Commander of SPLA Division 8, (with its headquarters in Pan-Pandiar near Bor in Jonglei state), declared on December 18, 2013 that he was no longer with the government.

General Peter Gatdeet's stated reason for rebellion was to avenge the killing of the Nuer in Juba by the Dinka. He had his Dinka colleagues exterminated in the Division and took over the state capital, Bor on December 18, 2013. Many Dinka civilians were reportedly massacred in the city including the sick and those who hid themselves in the churches and hospitals.

The 'Lou Nuer white army,' which was already organized by the opposition, moved through Bor town wreaking havoc as they headed towards South Sudan Capital Juba. The Dinka elements in Akobo, either in the army, other organized forces, or civil service were murdered. Others who tried to seek protection in UNMISS POC site in Akobo were also killed in cold blood right in front of UN forces there. The Nuer SPLA-IO elements in Akobo were blamed in the report by UN for inciting civilians to kill the Dinka (UNMISS, 2014; Pinaud, 2021).

On Decemeber 21, 2013, Division 4 Commander in Unity state Maj. Gen. James Koang Chol rebelled and joined forces with Dr. Riek Machar. He immediately declared himself as Caretaker Governor of Unity state. As a consequence, many Dinkas, both in the army and civil service were summarily executed. According to HRW (2014), UNMISS (2014) and Pinaud (2021), gross human rights violations were committed in Unity state capital Bentiu. This got worse on April 15, 2014 when more than 287 bodies of Darfuris were found inside and near the Mosque (Johnson, 2016). The reason for targeting

Darfuris was the alleged support their rebels rendered to the Government of South Sudan. In fact, incitements to kill non-Nuer in Bentiu, according to UNMISS (2014), were broadcasted on Bentiu radio in Nuer language.

The crisis of 2013 in Upper Nile state began in Nasir county on December 19, 2013. The white army in Nasir under the command of Gen. Gathoth Gatkuoth Hothnyang attacked the residence of their county Commissioner Dak Tap Chol. The skirmishes ended up with the destruction and looting of shops in Nasir town. The alleged reason for the assault was that the commissioner didn't support Dr. Riek Machar and that he protected the Dinka elements of the SPLA by taking them to UNMISS POC site.

On December 24, 2013, the war reached Malakal, capital of Upper Nile state. The city which was once a safe haven for those who fled from Juba was now engaged in military battle the like of which had never been seen before. The army and other organized forces in Malakal split into two groups along ethnic lines fighting against each other. In this battle of Malakal on December 24, I lost my four-year-old niece who fled from my home in Juba with her mother for safety in Upper Nile state. The mother carried her on her shoulders as they ran. For that reason, she also sustained a terrible injury in her neck, mouth and chin as the bullet which struck the baby dead also struck her.

After heavy fighting, the government forces were dislodged from town, but camped near the airport. After four days, the government troops regrouped and chased away the dissidents from town. Malakal town exchanged hands several times between government and rebels. The town was captured by rebels on December 24, 2013, then government forces captured it on December 28, 2013. Again the opposition took the town from the government forces on January 13, 2014. Again government on January 14, then opposition on January 19. Finally, the government took control from February 18 and retained it ever since.

Most government buildings and private homes were torched as the town changed hands between the government and the rebel forces on the dates indicated above. Thousands of people were killed in cold blood in the name of revenge. I visited the town on January 15, 2014. It was surreal! The destruction of Malakal town was indescribable.

The Nuer rebel forces, and the white army targeted the Dinka, the Chollo, the Mabanese, Nuer in government and others in the town of Malakal. This act of revenge became a serious predicament for the Nuer cause domestically and in-ternationally. As Pinaud (2021, p.148) stated, "The fact that the Nuer had violently retaliated after being massacred in Juba made the violence against them look ethnic than genocidal." The feeling of sympathy which the Nuer got from other ethnic groups in the country due to Juba massacre desiccated after the revenge. The killing of innocent people in Malakal generated too much hatred against the Nuer in Upper Nile.

It was the reason why the Maban Defense Force, a civilian militia group organized by a senior state government official from Maban county, killed Nuer civilians working for national and international humanitarian organizations in the county. The Chollo militia group organized by Gen. Johnson Olony known as 'Aguelek' engaged in killings and kidnappings of the Nuer people in government and those who sought refuge in

UNMISS POC site in Malakal. This action took place when the Nuer people tried to return to their homes from UNMISS POC site.

Even though he was a General in the SPLA, Johnson Olony and his Aguelek force attacked the home of then Upper Nile state Governor Simon Kun Puoc in 2015 to force the governor to rebel so that he could take over the governorship of the state. However, Gen. Johnson Olony was not reprimanded for such egregious action by the Government of South Sudan, which was in itself an indication that something was afoot with the command of the SPLA in this regard.

As a matter of fact, the Nuer in government, including state Governor Simon Kun Puoc, found it very difficult to live in Upper Nile. Some Dinka elements said that they could not protect a Nuer governor from Nuer rebels. For instance, when Malakal was under the rebel control, it was decided by the state administration that the seat of the state government would be relocated to Renk county in the north. The people and Members of Parliament from Renk county in the National Assembly vehemently rejected this proposal saying that they could not accept Simon Kun in their county. Their written position was published in the newspapers in Juba. In fact, the Nuer elements in South Sudan Police and other units of the organized forces were murdered earlier in cold blood in December 2013 by their Dinka colleagues in Renk county. In a way; therefore, the Nuer became the enemy of the state.

4.3. The Response of the Nuer in Government to the Crisis of December 15, 2013

As indicated elsewhere, the Nuer divided themselves into two groups early in late February 2013. One group supported Dr. Riek Machar's move and the other opposed it as a premature overture to snatch political power from a legitimately elected President.

The Nuer who did not join the opposition did not have a meeting to decide on how they would handle the crisis when it struck. However, (military or civilian) their actions were on one accord as though they had met. They played two important roles which included preservation of the unity of the country and protection of civilians caught in harm's way in various states in the country.

4.3.1. Preservation of the Unity of the Republic of South Sudan

Certain South Sudanese leaders do not understand the responsibilities which come with independence. These responsibilities require thorough analysis of issues prior to taking action which may undermine the existence and survival of the Republic. This is compounded by the fact that a large number of South Sudanese intellectuals were educated either outside the country or in religious institutions which did not offer training on building the national character of a person and the allegiance required to the State or country. Most of the times, they admired countries in which they lived or were educated rather than the one to which they belong.

Furthermore, some of the educated leaders in the government

and political parties in South Sudan are preoccupied with self-interest which they pursue almost at the expense of the welfare of the country. It is either their way or the highway. This demonstrates that even though independence might have been achieved on July 9, 2011, the need to preserve the sanctity of the Republic and self-sacrifice required for unity and general good of the nation were still in their primordial stages.

The moment the war started in December 2013, most leaders and people regressed into their ethnic cocoons for support. The idealism which brought about national unity during the liberation of the country hastily evaporated into thin air. The specter of tribalism engulfed the majority of our comrades in the country. Most were hypnotized by tribalism and jestered around tribal leaders for protection and comfort as national security institutions literally withered away. This was a testament to the fact that patriotism was feigned in the speeches and public mannerisms of the leaders of South Sudan. This lack of national devotion reached its anticlimactic ending on December 15, 2013 when only a few remained standing for South Sudan.

Majority of the Nuer politicians and leadership never left the Government of South Sudan. This was because of the belief that if all the Nuer left the Government of South Sudan, the country could have collapsed and degenerated into tribal fiefdoms. This was a situation which had to be avoided at all costs. If South Sudan collapsed, it was to be blamed on the Nuer generally even though not all of them participated in its near dismemberment and destruction.

Having the Nuer in big numbers in government demonstrated to the people of South Sudan and the world that the government was still a national government and not a Dinka enterprise, as those opposed portrayed it. Many Nuer leaders who did not have positions in government also remained in Juba to send strong message that they were still South Sudanese who must continue to live together. Their decision to stay in government also lessened the resolve of the Nuer white army to decimate the Republic of South Sudan. Even though under strenuous circumstances, the Nuer leaders in government have family members who listened to their advice. The white army knew that what the Nuer leaders in government stood for would prevail in the end over the message of revenge and regime change through violence.

Their strategy to focus on peace and reconciliation provided an alternative point of view from that of continuation of a senseless war by all sides. Though the urge to revenge was stronger than peaceful way of resolving the conflict, it became clear eventually that they were right and the civil population started to reduce their participation in the combat operations against the government, especially in the second half of 2014 in Upper Nile Region.

4.3.2. Protection of Civilians
in Harm's Way in Various States

When the war broke out on December 15, 2013, the Nuer scuttled to the homes of Nuer Ministers and Senior officers in the army and other organized forces for protection. These homes were not safe from the attackers, but at least they provided psychological relief for them.

What followed was to transport these people to UNMISS

POC sites for better security and protection. Many people flocked to my home in Mangateen. I had to transport them to UNMISS POC site in Thongpiny as did many Nuer leaders in Juba. For those who wanted to go to Khartoum, Kenya and Uganda, we provided either air tickets or chartered buses to take them.

Some Nuer expressed fear to live in Juba during the difficult days of the December crisis. Gen. James Hoth Mai, then SPLA Chief of General Staff and Maj. Gen. Simon Kun Puoc, then Governor of Upper Nile state, chartered flights to take them to Malakal as it was still safe at that time. After the Nuer went to UNMISS POC sites, there were constant attacks against them on the way whenever they tried to come to Juba town to work, shop or for any other reasons. The brand of this was carried by women who were allegedly assaulted sexually on the way. The Nuer in government addressed these challenges by engaging with the security sector to ensure safe passage and protection for them.

Another major protection operation was for us to assist those trapped in distant communities like Gurey, Jabel, etc., as well as those that hid themselves in ceilings, bushes and other places waiting for rescue. Whenever calls like this came, our officers would be sent to rescue those in harm's way.

This rescue operation involved everyone including our Dinka comrades and friends in the original SPLM/A and other organized forces. Comrades like, Maj. Gen. Marial Chinoung of Tiger, Maj. Gen. Mach Paul of SPLA MI, Maj. Gen. Akol Koor of NSS, and Gen. Pieng Deng Kuol, then Inspector General of South Sudan Police Service, just to mention, but a few who rescued the Nuer people from entrapment.

All appreciation was due to them as it was for then SPLA Chief of General Staff General James Hoth Mai, who was personally engaged in the rescue operations for those who were trapped. We were equally indebted to all our young officers and soldiers who sacrificed so much to rescue their brothers and sisters, mothers, and fathers in harm's way. While those who started the war ran to save their lives, those who remained were the true patriots protecting the most vulnerable in a situation of enormous adversity. Had they run away, thousands more could have lost their lives.

Our work to protect people from harm's way did not end with the Nuer in Juba. There were many Dinka comrades who were in danger in various military units in Unity, Upper Nile, and Jonglei states.

In Nasir county, Dak Tap Chol, who was then Nasir county Commissioner, refused to support the rebellion of Dr. Riek Machar and took Dinka elements of the SPLA unit in Nasir town to UNMISS POC site. This was the reason why he was attacked by the civil population as they were being enflamed by some Nuer leaders from the area who supported Dr. Riek Machar.

In Ulang county, we engaged our local population with telephones to spare the Dinka in the SPLA unit there. The then Ulang county Commissioner Gatkuoth Biem Nyok, together with the local Chiefs managed to safeguard the Dinka in the SPLA unit there. However, one weakness prevailed in the situation of Ulang. There was no UNMISS POC site in the county. The nearest UNMISS post was in Nasir town and there was no way these people could have been taken there without being intercepted by those who wanted to eliminate them.

Though the civil population wasn't involved, the internal fractionation within the SPLA unit caught up with them and ended in tragedy.

The situation in Maiwut county was similar to that of Ulang in that there was no UNMISS POC site there. But Maiwut is a border county with Ethiopia. The then Maiwut county Commissioner Paul Biel Chol, 2nd Lt. Deng Puot Deng and I were engaged with commander of the SPLA unit in the area Col. David Mut to ensure that his Dinka comrades were not murdered in cold blood by the civilians. During this time, 2nd Lt. Deng Puot came to Juba from Ethiopia to give his report to his supervisors when the tragedy of 2013 struck the country.

David Mut had not defected yet at that time, so he listened to our advice. He instructed Colonel Biel Thomas who was an MI officer to contact Ambassador Arop Deng Kuol in Addis-Ababa to organize an evacuation plan for those soldiers and their families. We told David that he should send all the Dinka comrades in his unit across Pagak Bridge to the Ethiopian side where they would be extracted by Ethiopian security forces whom we had spoken with earlier. During the day, 2nd Lt Deng Puot Deng spoke with General Mohammed Yonis popularly known as 'Samora,' the then Ethiopian Army Chief of General Staff, about the possibility of extracting SPLA personnel in the Ethiopian side of Pagak whose lives were under threat. Gen. Somora agreed that if they crossed the border to the Ethiopian side, he would be able to assist.

The Dinka, including their Nuer wives, were more than 500 in number and Col. David Mut and Col. Biel Thomas took them across the bridge as we discussed. South Sudan Ambassador in Addis Ababa H.E Arop Deng Kuol did an excellent job in

Addis-Ababa by "by making contribution to charter buses to transport the Dinka soldiers from Pagak bridge to safety in the Ethiopian side" (Kuol, et al., 2020, p.133). The Ethiopian authorities took them to Makot Airport in Gambella. The SPLA headquarters in Juba chartered a flight and 2nd Lt. Deng Puot Deng took the plane to Ethiopia and brought them to safety in Juba. The knowledge and connections of our colleagues in Ethiopia made it possible for us to rescue our Dinka comrades from the jaws of death.

As soon as the first group arrived in Juba with their families, one Lt. Col. came to see me to express their collective gratitude for the miracle of saving their lives. In fact, it was the first time for me to see their leader, the Lt. Colonel, who was deputy of Col. David Mut in Maiwut. Some Dinka in Unity state were also allowed to leave for nearby states secretly by their friends in uniform and the same happened in Fangak county.

4.3.3. The Nuer in the SPLM and Government: The Price of Patriotism

Remaining loyal to the Government of South Sudan and SPLM for reasons stated earlier was a litmus test. The price was too great for those who committed ourselves to the cause of South Sudan. The fact that we rose above the demise of our people did not mean that we were unscathed by the agony of their death. We lost sisters, brothers, relatives, and close friends. We were very much affected psychologically, perhaps a little more than those who heard the rumours of the massacre.

Standing for the unity and interest of the country in an ethnically charged environment like South Sudan in 2013 was very challenging. On the one hand, logic and reason dictate that we are all South Sudanese and our allegiance should be to all our people in the country regardless of their ethnicity. But, on the other hand, one also belongs to a particular ethnic group just like the other leaders who stand in support of their ethnic bases. The two loyalties should naturally complement each other as they are mutually reinforcing. But this has not been the case in South Sudan where conflict proliferated along ethnic lines. Supporting the interest of the country at the apparent expense of one's ethnic interest was uncommon, and it made others question our mental equanimity.

For us, logic and patriotism dictate that our people are the people of South Sudan as a whole, not just the Nuer. We were troubled by the way our people were killing each other in the country in various locations. We know that the Nuer were killed and so were other South Sudanese in the Nuer areas. Our concern was to end the war quickly before it could destroy even more lives. We were mindful that the proliferation of a senseless war in Upper Nile was going to snowball into other regions of the country as more politicians, who did not see themselves in the next reshuffle of Government of South Sudan, were poised to join the opposition in an effort to be part of the power-sharing arrangement being discussed in Addis-Ababa.

But, that thinking was an exception rather than the norm. It became so unorthodox that its validity was questioned by many Nuer and leaders from other ethnic groups as being too utopian. For taking such a stand, we were disowned and isolated by both sides to the conflict. The Nuer community known as BNFA (Bentiu, Nasir, Fangak and Akobo districts) deleted our names from the community list as in their view, 'We became Dinka' since we did not support their cause.

It could have made sense if the government and majority

of our Dinka colleagues in power reciprocated our patriotic resolve and standpoint. However, recognition and support from the Government of South Sudan and the SPLM, was almost non-existent at that time. Even an acknowledgement of our role as stated previously, by the government could have made the difference. Instead, the government isolated us with the exception of new found SPLM Nuer members who were originally from NCP. Some elements in the government thought we did not leave because we were trapped. They assumed we were waiting for Machar to take over power so that we could join him. They totally misunderstood our resolve and commitment to this country and the SPLM. We remained here for South Sudan and not for anything else.

Appointments to senior government positions came and went and not a single one of us was appointed. There were various national committees established, such as the Crisis Management and Peace Committees, to assist and support peace in the Nuer areas destroyed by war in 2014. Logic could have dictated that if these committees were to engage with the Nuer civil population, it could have been reasonable to have Nuer in them. However, the Nuer were excluded from the membership of these high committees established by the President. It was only in the sub-committees that some Nuer were co-opted by their friends who headed the committees. Peace talks in Addis-Ababa excluded the Nuer of Upper Nile and Unity states. It was not accidental that the state governorships of those states were given away in the agreement to Riek Machar's opposition.

For the majority of our Dinka brothers and sisters, we were 'Nuer' and nothing else. The fact that our presence legitimized the Government of South Sudan which they lead couldn't come close to the mind of those running the government. Our state of affairs in government was in jeopardy confirming what my friend at the United Nations Office in South Sudan told me in December 2013 that, 'The political victims of this war would be the Nuer patriots because they belonged to nobody but the country.'

The Nuer in opposition fumed with anger towards us for not supporting the cause of Dr. Riek Machar or joining them in the war of revenge. In fact, they could not get their heads around the reason why we refused to join them. They said that we were bought by Dinka to stay aloof from the war. Hence, they coined the term 'Nuer wew' to describe us, or as Pendle (2020) put it frankly, 'Nuer of Dinka Money.' For them, we became their enemy number one. In their social media writings and video postings where they incite the Nuer to revenge and kill the Dinka, they never missed the opportunity to take a swipe at us, 'We will get you. We will kill you first before the Dinkas.'

By way of anecdote, the following message may clarify the level of their anger. I got a Facebook message on December 16, 2013 from a Nuer woman in America who was a longtime friend. She wrote, 'I wish the Dinka people kill you Peter Lam Both …you are lucky, if you were my husband, I would kill you right now.' The timing of this message couldn't have been more critical. It was during this time the killing of the Nuer people from house to house was at its peak in Juba, including in my neighbourhood of Mangateen.

She wrote this to me because she sent out earlier in the day a picture of a small baby on Facebook whose chin and mouth were blown away by bullet in Juba, allegedly by a Dinka. She used this picture as an instrument to incite the Nuer to revenge the death of this baby. I wrote to her inbox that 'Pictures of such kind were fueling the fight and that they were not helping us to stop the war.' Her response demonstrated the level of anger and hatred the Nuer in opposition had for us.

In our case, the reasons for our refusal to join them in the war were simple. Dr. Riek Machar and his associates were fighting to return to their previous positions in government. We did not view it as a reasonable cause to destroy our country. Secondly, the revenge for those killed in Juba cannot be a reason to destroy the country as there were legal avenues to seek justice for them. It was incumbent upon us to make a choice between our emotional state and reason. The urge to revenge was an emotional response to the crisis. We believed that it was not reasonable to kill our people and destroy our country for that cause. This decision was based on conscientious judgement though some critics questioned our mental equability.

Nevertheless, I was soothed by an email I got on December 19, 2013. The message was from a Dinka girl in Melbourne, Australia. I went to Australia in September 2010 at the invitation of South Sudanese there to discuss preparations for the referendum and what their role would be in that country.

During that time, I was Deputy National Secretary for External Affairs in the SPLM in addition to being a Minister of Information and Broadcasting in the Upper Nile state Government. I held a briefing meeting with SPLM members in Melbourne to this effect and some of them took my contacts. This girl might have been one of those who kept my contacts. So, she wrote to me these words: "Hon. Peter Lam Both, thank you for not running away from Juba. I know your relatives are killed, but please keep our country together."

At first glance, I thought it was a simple message, but then, I contemplated on it deeply in relation to many messages posted on social media, especially that Facebook message from my longtime Nuer friend in America. I meditated on this, "If I and many Nuer leaders ran away, who could have saved the lives of the Nuer people trapped in violence in Juba? If I had run away, who could have saved some of our Dinka brothers and sisters trapped in the Nuer land? If I had run away, who could have stood for the Republic of South Sudan? If I had run away, who could have stood for the SPLM?" I became happy because that young lady understood the true meaning of patriotism and its concomitant sacrifices. I wrote back to her and said, 'Thank you…. please do the same in Australia.' Her message comforted me. Little things like these encourage people to do the right things.

CHAPTER FIVE

***

The Regional Mediation
Through IGAD

SOUTH SUDAN'S FREEDOM was attained and cemented by the blood of the martyrs with the material and moral support from so many countries including IGAD member States who mediated the Comprehensive Peace Agreement that ended the war and made the independence of South Sudan possible. For this reason, these countries have a vested interest in the internal affairs of South Sudan.

During the celebration on Independence Day on July 9, 2013, the President of Uganda, H.E Yoweri Kaguta Museveni was one of the dignitaries that attended the occasion. In fact, he never missed these celebrations in South Sudan. He was always given a chance to address the people of South Sudan on behalf of other foreign dignitaries.

On this day, Dr. Machar came first as usual to the celebration site at Dr. John Garang Mausoleum. When President Museveni arrived, Dr. Riek Machar went to receive and usher him to his seat. While doing so, Dr. Riek Machar opened his hands to give him the famous 'Sudanese hug.' But Museveni thwarted the hug and went for a cold handshake. I was intently watching what was unfolding. It was a sign that something was afoot with President Museveni. Some senior members of the SPLM including its Secretary General did not turn up in the celebration. When President Museveni spoke, he said three things which made me believe that war was inevitable in South Sudan and that Uganda might play some role in it. He said:

> There is a saying in Uganda that if you have opening between your teeth, you cannot eat meat very well. If you are holding a stick in your hands, don't let someone take it from you and hit you with it first. If someone killed your father, you cannot allow him to sleep with your mother.

After hearing these things, I said to my wife, who was sitting next to me that, 'We already have a war in our country.' She asked me why. I said because the man with the diastema is Dr. Riek Machar. He was not satisfied with what he has as Vice President. That is compared with not eating meat well when one has an opening between his/her teeth. President Kiir has a stick which he must use against Dr. Riek Machar and those who opposed him before they could use it against him. And finally, Dr. Machar almost killed the SPLM/A in 1991 (the father), how could he now want to lead a party (sleeping with the mother) which was only sustained by others?

Indeed, when the war started on December 15, 2013, Ugandan military landed in Juba on December 18, 2013 to help secure and protect the capital from the marauding Nuer white army. The Ugandan forces effectively bombarded the Nuer white army from the air and ground. The coming of Ugandan forces to South Sudan was allegedly sanctioned by certain regional bodies as well as some western powers after they saw the destruction in Bor, Malakal and Bentiu towns by the Nuer white army. Those foreign powers realized that it was no longer a political war with a national agenda. The war had civilian element bent on destroying towns and killing people as they avenged the Nuer killed in Juba.

There were reports that the SPLA-N and Justice and Equality Movement (JEM) of Darfur (Johnson, 2016) also entered the war in support of the government, especially in Upper Nile and Unity states. It was said that in Unity state, the JEM fighters were seen with the SPLA when they captured Bentiu. In Upper Nile, there were reports about the SPLA-N coming from Blue Nile and Nuba Mountains into Malakal with the government troops.

This information was predominantly from the rebel sources as they courted the support of the Sudan and Ethiopian Governments. In fact, the Government of Sudan supported them with military equipment and training in Bouth (Southern Blue Nile state) where they launched attacks against government positions in Renk and Maban counties of Upper Nile state.

The support of Ethiopia to the opposition was limited to allowing them to enter their country either to live there or permit their logistics to proceed to their base in Pagak, South

Sudan. Their biggest support base was the Ethiopian Nuer in Gambella Region. In fact, the Regional Government of Gambella and its people were hostile to the Government of South Sudan. It was a no go area for the Government of South Sudan officials. If anyone dared to enter, they were arrested and deported to Pagak where Dr. Riek Machar and his forces were or jailed in Gambella. The Gambella Nuer provided the opposition with logistics and everything else, including their physical participation in the war on the side of Dr. Riek Machar. These people did not even realize that they were citizens of another country and that their participation in another country's civil war could jeopardize relations between South Sudan and Ethiopia and this might have been their prime objective.

5.1. The IGAD Mediation Process

When war broke out on December 15, 2013, the world was stunned by the event. They could not understand what went wrong in a young country which was so jubilant on Independence Day. The same feeling was displayed by South Sudanese who were outside the political circles in Juba. However, the events leading to the unfortunate day of December 15, 2013 were not surprising to the leaders of the country. Foreign embassies in Juba including the UN Mission in South Sudan were worried and wrote messages to their headquarters expressing concern that South Sudan was headed for war.

As soon as fighting broke out in South Sudan, General Lazarus Sumbyeiwo of Kenya arrived in Juba on December 18, 2013 to inquire on how he could help. The following day, Foreign Ministers from the region came to Juba led by then Ethiopian

Minister of Foreign Affairs Dr. Theodros Adhanom. They too wanted to salvage the situation before it escalated further.

Their return to their capitals ushered a quick response to restore peace and stability through the mechanism of Intergovernmental Authority on Development (IGAD). The Member States of IGAD, Troika, IGAD Partners Forum, African Union and United Nations supported the peace initiative. Donald Booth, then US Special Envoy for South Sudan and Sudan, arrived in Juba and discussed the issues of peace and the release of the detainees. The international community did not buy the coup theory. They believed the opposition politicians were detained for their political views rather than involvement in a criminal activity or *coup d'état*.

On December 28, 2013, the 23rd Extraordinary IGAD Summit on South Sudan crisis was convened in Nairobi. Then Foreign Minister Barnaba Marial Benjamin attended on behalf of the Government of South Sudan. Neither President Salva Kiir nor Dr. Riek Machar attended that summit. When the communiqué was published, it condemned any attempt to change the Government of South Sudan through unconstitutional means (communiqué, 2013).

Many political observers were surprised by this statement. On the one hand, the world said there was no coup, but on the other hand, they released a statement condemning it. This would not be the only paradox in the IGAD mediation process. In this summit, IGAD appointed three Special Envoys for South Sudan and they were General Lazarus Sumbeiywo of Kenya, Mohammed Ahmed Mustafa Al Dhabi of Sudan and Ambassador Seyum Mesfin, a long-serving former Ethiopian Foreign minister.

5.1.1. The Response of the Government and Rebels to IGAD Mediation Initiative

In December 2013, IGAD presented the negotiating teams with a Road Map for Peace in South Sudan. After this session, the rebels and government teams returned to their bases to brief their principals on the road map for peace and get their directives for the next round.

On the government side, President Kiir called a meeting of senior members of the government and SPLM to deliberate on the road map. The government consultative meeting took place in J-1 in Juba. A heated discussion took place. Almost all the attendants were opposed to the road map as it gave Riek Machar and his group, the position of Executive Prime Minister with powers which were reserved for the President by the Transitional Constitution of South Sudan.

As a matter of fact, President Kiir was elected in 2010 as an Executive President and any move that would strip him of his people-given powers was perceived as an act of usurpation. Therefore, the government negotiation team was empowered to return to Addis-Ababa to negotiate in such spirit.

On the rebel side, Riek Machar called for a conference of the opposition in Pagak, Maiwut county, Upper Nile state, to deliberate on the road map. On January 12, 2014, the armed opposition came up with the following resolutions according to an insider's report:

1. *The SPLM/A-IO agreed in principle to negotiate peace with the Government of South Sudan;*
2. *The SPLM/A-IO shall stay separate during the*

Transitional Period for three years. They shall have their own separate command and Chief of General Staff;

3. *There shall be President without Vice President;*

4. *There shall be an Executive Prime Minister without any deputy;*

5. *Power-sharing between the SPLM/A-IO and the SPLM in Government must be 50-50;*

6. *The armed forces that shall stay in Juba must be Joint Integrated Units between the rebel forces and the government forces. Both sides shall contribute 50-50 to the force that shall be stationed in Juba;*

7. *The name SPLM/A-IO shall NOT be changed. Any change must come after the Transitional period;*

8. *They resolved to continue fighting the government until a comprehensive peace was signed;*

9. *White army leaders must be promoted to the ranks of Brigadiers General. The white army must be the auxiliary force that shall fight side by side with the SPLM/A-IO forces;*

10. *They resolved to continue fighting the Government of South Sudan despite the ceasefire agreement signed by the two principals;*

11. *The rebel commanders (Peter Gatdeet, James Koang Chol, Dau Aturjong, Tanginye, Simon Gatwech Dual, Gathoth Gatkuoth) would go to Khartoum after Pagak Conference to solicit military support to continue fighting;*

12. *Gen. Dau Aturjong was instructed to open Bahr El Ghazal Front from Northern Bahr El Ghazal and fight*

his way to Warrap state. The same instruction was given to Peter Gatdeet to open a new front to Warrap through Unity state;

13. *Gen. Alfred Lado Gore was instructed to organize Equatorians and Nuer fighters to disrupt Nimule and Kenya trade routes and other important roads that supplied Juba. He was encouraged that he did not need any fighting force. They were encouraged to carry out hit and run attack and the trade between Juba and Uganda would collapse; and*

14. *Dr. Riek Machar was asked to remain in Pagak until he organized the rebels into an organized fighting force to disrupt those trade routes. At that time, each commander operated independently without any command structure.*

As gathered from the above rebel resolutions, their position was not different from that of the government. They also rejected the road map with little room to maneuver. After Pagak Conference, clashes started on the Juba-Nimule road in which some vehicles were destroyed. Indeed, instability started to increase in Central, Eastern and Western Equatoria states as military activities multiplied.

In fact, some senior state officials in Eastern, Central and Western Equatoria began to be suspected by national security service as being sympathetic to the rebels, especially in regard to their call for federalism; which was concurrently demanded by the rebels. However, federalism had always been a call by Greater Equatoria politicians prior to the crisis in the country. As a matter of fact, it could be argued that Dr. Riek Machar added the demand for federalism to his political agenda just to attract Equatorians to join his movement.

The efforts of IGAD mediated peace talks resulted in the signing of the Agreement on Cessation of Hostilities on January 23, 2014 in Addis-Ababa between the Government of South Sudan and SPLM in opposition. The agreement was to enter into force 24 hours after its signature by the parties and witnessed by IGAD Special Envoys. However, as the events on the ground showed, this agreement was violated before the ink dried on the papers.

The rebels under Dr. Riek Machar included civilians or white army which was not entirely under his command and control. At the same time, the SPLA forces on the ground were non-committal to the Cessation of Hostilities Agreement. Therefore, the agreement shriveled from the pages as soon as it was inked.

As there was no mechanism to monitor the violations of ceasefire, IGAD would resort to condemning both sides every time there was a violation. It frustrated the Government of South Sudan to the point where it resorted to writing protest letters to IGAD as to why the agency would condemn both parties for violations when the culprit was known.

The rebels also protested the same approach. In fact, the SPLM/A-IO got better at this. If they were ready to attack any government position, they would instruct their spokesperson to release a press statement that they were attacked today in this or that place by the government. The next day, the SPLM/A-IO would launch an attack and call it self-defense from yesterday's government offensive which they feigned. IGAD had no idea who did what first. The war propaganda got the better of the world for there was no monitoring and evaluation mechanism in the field.

Before the next round of negotiations in Addis-Ababa, the Government of South Sudan, under intense pressure from the international community, decided to release seven political detainees. They were taken to Kenya under that government's auspices. Those who remained in detention included Pa'gan Amum, Gen. Oyay Deng Ajak, Gen. Dr. Majak de Agot and Ambassador Ezekiel Lol Gatkuoth to await trail, but only to be released on April 24, 2014 when the government ordered the 'stay' of the criminal proceedings at the request of the political leadership that had an interest in the case.

However, the government witnesses failed their own case. Maj. Gen. Mach Paul, then SPLA's Chief Military Intelligence Officer in his deposition stated that there was no coup attempt and the man who arrested the detainees Aleu Ayieny Aleu, then Minister of Interior, refused to testify before the court. The testimony by some personnel of other law enforcement agencies to support the coup theory was not sufficient to warrant conviction. Hence, the detainees were released. It was a great mortification for the Government of South Sudan.

On March 3, 2014, the parties to the conflict signed the matrix for implementation of the Cessation of Hostilities Agreement in the hope that this time around, it might actually work. But, nothing much changed as violations of the agreement continued relentlessly.

On March 13, 2014, the IGAD Summit focused on the need for an inclusive dialogue where political detainees, other political parties, civil society, youth and women groups would be represented in the negotiations. In the first instance, both the SPLM/A-IO and the government rejected this approach stating the obvious that the negotiations could be diluted by views that might not reflect the interest of the actual belligerents.

IGAD resisted that notion and expressed concern about a narrow approach to peace which could not address the fundamental and immediate causes of the conflict. In the end, all the stakeholders participated. However, inclusivity or any other method, did not prevent the violation of Cessation of Hostilities Agreement by the belligerents. On April 28, 2014, both President Kiir and Dr. Riek Machar attended the IGAD Summit and committed themselves in a signed communiqué to end the hostilities with immediate effect. The commitment of the two principals on paper did not produce any positive results on the ground.

In May 2014 fighting exacerbated and this prompted IGAD on 10 June Summit to compel the leaders of SPLM/A-IO and government to end all hostilities and form the Transitional Government of National Unity within 60 days which fell on August 10, 2014. That deadline elapsed without any agreement. This was because both leaders had hardliners on their bases which forced them to retract from what they agreed to do once they arrived at their headquarters. This deadline could not be met, and neither was another extension.

5.1.2. The Crisis Within IGAD Mediation

Michael Makuei Lueth, Minister of Information of the Government of South Sudan and official spokesman of the government negotiation team, always returned from Addis-Ababa's IGAD peace talks with funny phrases like, 'Peace is at the corner! It is now at the door! This is unbecoming referring to IGAD mediation! The mediators needed mediation! etc.' This showed the difficulty with the mediation process as it was also reflective of the interests of the mediators. The conflict of interest among the mediators postured a serious crisis within the IGAD mediation process. South Sudanese were not allowed to deliberate among themselves directly to find durable peace. The mediators were the ones moving between the government and the opposition negotiating teams to collect information which would then be presented as basis for an agreement. Such an approach and the interest of specific IGAD countries in South Sudan affairs complicated the process of negotiation as shown below.

Uganda

Uganda is one of the countries which heavily supported the SPLM/A during the liberation struggle through provision of military hardware and training. When South Sudan became independent, the SPLM government tried to return the favour by starting negotiations to end the conflict in northern Uganda led by Joseph Konyi of Lord's Resistance Army (LRA). Konyi was an internationally wanted person by the International Criminal Court (ICC) due to alleged crimes he committed in northern Uganda. The US, Uganda and other powers were poised to arrest him, but to no avail. However, the Government of South Sudan, through the office of the then Vice President of the Government of southern Sudan Dr. Riek Machar started contacts with him to start the process of peace.

This intervention by Vice President of the Government of

southern Sudan was resisted internationally because Konyi was considered as international criminal with whom governments should not negotiate. However, Dr. Riek Machar and the southern Sudan Government insisted that a peaceful approach needed to be given a chance. Therefore, the Vice President proceeded with that initiative even though it ended up in fiasco when Konyi killed his chief negotiator Vincent Otti on October 2, 2007 and then disappeared into the Garamba forest in Democratic Republic of Congo (DRC).

International security analysts wondered whether Konyi used the southern Sudan mediation initiative as a way to relocate his forces and escape into hiding in DRC. The African Union's Regional Cooperation Initiative for elimination of LRA (RCI-LRA) had been successful in killing and denying territory for LRA fighters (www.peaceau.org>page>100>au-led-rci-lra-1).

Countries in the region such as Uganda, South Sudan, DRC and Central African Republic (CAR) contributed to the RCI-LRA's taskforce. This regional effort was complimented by international support and as a result, LRA was declared non-effective though its leader Joseph Konyi remained at large.

Uganda also considered South Sudan as a strategic partner. It was the first country which sent its troops into South Sudan on December 18, 2013 to protect important government installations and actively participated in combat operations in Jonglei using air and ground forces. Since 2005, Uganda has had a very large population living and working in South Sudan. The country also exported much of its agricultural and other products to South Sudan. Since the time of the liberation struggle, Uganda has been hosting southern Sudanese refugees and even after independence, families of South Sudanese continue to live and study in the country. As a result, the Ugandan economy benefited from remittances by South Sudanese to their families.

During the negotiation process, Uganda got frustrated by the intransigence of South Sudanese belligerents, especially the Government of President Salva Kiir. It was rumoured that President Museveni was interested in someone from Equatoria for the presidency of South Sudan as it became clear that Nuer and Dinka did not listen to advice from him and other regional leaders.

During his meeting with the Former Detainees (FDs) on April 9, 2017, he accused the leadership of South Sudan of saying that the country was liberated by Dinkas only. This was because many leaders from Dinka community, including members of the SPLM political bureau uttered these words in several meetings which sometimes were broadcasted on national SSTV and radio. For this reason, President Museveni had this admonition for Dinka leadership in the Government of South Sudan:

> *Meles Zinawi (late Ethiopian Prime Minister), Isaias Afwerki (Eritrean President) and myself, fought and shed blood in Sudan and compelled Beshir on the table to accept self-determination and independence for the people of South Sudan. Now there is this claim that only the Dinkas liberated South Sudan. Were we also Dinkas? What about 98.83 per cent voters in the referendum who endorsed your independence and those Americans and Europeans who supported you? Were they all Dinkas?*

This statement from the President of Uganda carried more than an admonition. It could also mark a new chapter in the Uganda-South Sudan relations in the future if the direction the Government of South Sudan had taken did not change. It is not accidental that General Thomas Cirilo Swaka's National Salvation Front (NAS) movement has an official office in Kampala.

Ethiopia

Ethiopia has a long history of relations with South Sudan (Both, 2003). The Anya Nya, Anya Nya II and SPLM/A were all supported by Ethiopian people and their governments. The country housed a large number of refugees from southern Sudan for years during the national liberation struggle. Ethiopia was one of the countries which vigorously supported the independence of South Sudan in 2011 by the leadership of Ethiopian People's Revolutionary Democratic Front (EPRDF) under then Prime Minister Meles Zinawi.

After independence, Ethiopia saw itself as one of the most important strategic allies of the young Republic. South Sudan also hosted a large number of Ethiopians living and working in South Sudan. They invested in hotel and restaurant businesses. Besides, Ethiopia has a Nuer population in their country especially in the Gambella region which could foster positive relations between the two countries. However, the Ethiopian Nuer were very hostile to the Government of South Sudan after the Nuer massacre in December 2013.

In Gambella, the Nuer did not want anyone who supported the Government of South Sudan in their region even when the Ethiopian government allowed that person to visit. It was feared that their support could sway Ethiopia's resolve to stay neutral from the conflict in South Sudan. However, it was in the best interest of the two countries to have peace in South Sudan to enhance their bilateral interests.

When the conflict erupted in the country, then Ethiopian Foreign Minister Dr. Theodros Adhanom led the first IGAD Foreign Ministers' delegation to Juba on December 19, 2013 to acquaint themselves with the situation and to examine what role they could play to resolve it.

The delegation of Ethiopian Foreign Minister came a day after General Lazarus Sumbyeiwo of Kenya arrived in Juba. This later complicated the mediation process as Ethiopia and Kenya competed for venue of the talks and the leadership of the mediation process.

Many analysts were of the opinion that the head of the mediation could have been General Sumbyeiwo who negotiated the Comprehensive Peace Agreement because he gained experience with the process and the people affected. However, Ethiopia's Ambassador Seyum Mesfin became IGAD's Chief negotiator. According to Johnson (2016), such a title never existed and no one knew how it came about. But, that was how Ethiopia took both the Chair and the venue of the mediation process to the disappointment of Kenya.

In fact, I was in Addis-Ababa when some disagreement emerged between Ambassador Seyum and Gen. Sumbyeiwo over the text of the proposed agreement. What was agreed in the talks was allegedly changed by the Chief Negotiator to suit the interest of certain western powers to the point where the latter returned to Kenya in frustration. He had to be convinced to return to the mediation process by his President.

This political wrangling between Kenya and Ethiopia complicated the mediation to the point where Michael Makuei Lueth, South Sudan's Minister of Information and official spokesman of the government's negotiating team had to utter these words on SSTV and radio that, 'The mediators needed mediating,' a point which Johnson (2016) emphasized.

Kenya

Kenya, as a neighbour, supported the SPLM/A during the liberation struggle by hosting the families of SPLM/A senior Commanders, especially after the fall of the Dergue regime in Ethiopia on May 28, 1991 when the SPLM/A was ousted by the new government led by the new ruling party, Ethiopian People's Revolutionary Democratic Front (EPRDF). The country was also the convener and the host of CPA negotiations for over a decade.

Large numbers of southern Sudanese refugees during the liberation struggle sought asylum in Kenya. For these reasons, the newly established Government of southern Sudan in 2006 donated to Kenya $1million dollars as its first humanitarian assistance to a foreign country.

Much of the interest of Kenya after the independence of South Sudan is rooted in their heavy investment in the banking and financial architecture of the country. Besides, Kenya contributed troops to United Nations Mission in South Sudan (UNMISS) and its General was appointed as Force Commander for the mission. He served until after the J-1 incident of July 8, 2016 where he was blamed for not doing enough to protect civilians. The Deputy head of Joint Monitoring and Evaluation

Commission (JMEC) which was tasked to monitor the implementation of ARCSS was from Kenya. After the revitalization process, the Chair of Revitalized Joint Monitoring and Evaluation Commission (R-JMEC) also went to Kenya.

Since the country's education system is still in its infancy, the majority of South Sudanese people still use Kenya for education of their children. This has helped Kenya to boost its economy through remittances of hard currency to the country from South Sudan. It is therefore in the best interest of Kenya that South Sudan becomes peaceful again. It was in this light that the country dispatched General Sumbeiywo to South Sudan on December 18, 2013 to search for ways to stop the conflict. Their interest to lead and host the negotiations led to unnecessary friction with Ethiopia as the two struggled for dominance. This delayed the resolution of conflict in South Sudan.

Sudan

The sisterly country of Sudan had been vacillating in its approach to South Sudan crisis. On the one hand, it was part of IGAD mediation, and its Special Envoy played an important role in the process. However, it was opposed to Uganda's military presence in South Sudan. There was fear that Sudan could support the group of Dr. Riek Machar militarily if Uganda continued to stay in South Sudan. During the liberation struggle, Sudan and Uganda accused each other of supporting their rebel groups. This historical grudge could easily resurface in South Sudan's conflict thereby spiraling it into a regional war.

The Government of South Sudan was accused by the SPLM/A-IO of employing SPLM-N and Justice and Equality

Movement (JEM) of Darfur of fighting against them. Whether it was true or not, the Sudan could easily accuse the Government of South Sudan of providing support to the Sudanese rebel groups. That government could assume that the participation of the Sudanese rebels on the side of South Sudan was a demonstration of their gratitude for provision of such support. As a matter of fact, the Sudan Government provided military and training support to the SPLM/A-IO of Dr. Riek Machar. Johnson (2016) observed that there were substantial indications that Sudan and Iran were providing direct military support while the State of Qatar contributed financially to the SPLM/A-IO.

Nevertheless, the cabinet of the Government of South Sudan which was appointed on 31 July 2013 carried the day. It was comprised of former senior members of the National Congress Party (NCP) who worked closely with President El Beshir in the Sudan Government during the liberation struggle. The Government of Sudan was delighted to see friendly faces in the cabinet of South Sudan. President Beshir's administration hoped that their presence in the Government of South Sudan would improve bilateral relations between the two countries now that the SPLM die-hards were out of the picture.

In fact, their existence improved bilateral relations between Juba and Khartoum. Later on, President Beshir and President Salva Kiir visited their capitals as a gesture of positive relations. It was this relationship, cushioned by the presence of Khartoum friendly faces in the Government of South Sudan, that diminished Sudan's resolve to support Dr. Riek Machar's group overtly and heavily.

With the IGAD countries having conflicting interests in South Sudan, the mediation process was complicated. That was partly the reason why the final agreement had to be imposed on the parties by IGAD-Plus Group. It was one of the few experiences where the mediators had to craft an agreement and force the parties to the conflict to accept it without any amendment. In this way, the IGAD mediation represented another level of hurdle which delayed the achievement of peace in South Sudan.

5.1.3. Parallel Mediation Process: The SPLM Reunification Endeavor

The war in South Sudan started as a result of a power struggle within the SPLM leadership. Dr. Riek Machar, Rebecca Nyandeng de Mabior and Pa'gan Amum made their intentions clear that they wanted to challenge Salva Kiir Mayardit in the race for the position of the Chairperson in the SPLM. Prof. Dr. James Wani Igga hinted that if Salva Kiir stepped down, he would consider running for the highest office in the party. This struggle happened because the Chairperson of the SPLM would ultimately become the flag bearer of the party during the general elections scheduled for June 2015.

The potential candidates saw the preparation process of the basic documents of the SPLM as a golden opportunity to write them in their favour. When it became clear in the NLC meeting of December 14-15, 2013, that the documents were approved in favour of the incumbent Chairman, crisis started in the night of December 15, 2013. In this regard, the schism of December 2013 was a failure of the SPLM leadership to resolve their political differences using the structures of the party.

As a result, friendly countries demonstrated their interest

to reconcile and reunite the fractured SPLM leadership in the hope that it could provide the necessary impetus for the stalled IGAD peace talks in Addis-Ababa. African National Congress (ANC) of South Africa, EPRDF of Ethiopia and Chama Cha Mapinduzi (CCM) of Tanzania took the initiative to bring the SPLM leadership together. The EPRDF hosted the opening meeting in Addis-Ababa in which senior members of the SPLM, SPLM-FDs and SPLM-IO were in attendance.

It was then decided that the venue of the meeting would be shifted to Tanzania as Ethiopia was more focused on IGAD peace talks. This process in its own right was daunting as the genesis of South Sudan's crisis was in the SPLM. The CCM of Tanzania took the lead and Arusha became the venue for the discussion of the SPLM reunification.

The SPLM sent a team to Arusha which consisted of per-sonalities who were ready to unify the party. The rebel team also consisted of responsible leaders. The process was mediation in the true meaning of the term.

Both groups of SPLM were allowed to dialogue and discuss directly among themselves with Tanzanian and South African teams intervening only when it was necessary to break any deadlock between the belligerent parties. As a result of their efforts, the SPLM Arusha Declaration was signed on January 26, 2015 by President Salva Kiir, Dr. Riek Machar and Pa'gan Amum who represented the three splinter groups of the SPLM.

The Arusha Declaration resolved most of the conten-tious issues which brought about the split in December 2013. Regarding the voting method, it was agreed that for con-troversial issues, a secret ballot would be utilized whereas for non-controversial issues, a show of hands would be the appropriate method. For the 5% quota for the representation of the minorities, it was agreed that the SPLM's Political Bureau was to develop a mechanism for their representation rather than giving the Chairman responsibility to appoint them. It was further agreed that the SPLM would develop a succession plan and retirement packages for senior cadres.

The Arusha Declaration called for Former Detainees (FDs) also known as G-10 and SPLM/A-IO of Dr. Riek Machar to return to Juba for its implementation. However, these two groups could not go to Juba immediately fearing for their personal safety. This was especially true for Dr. Riek Machar and his group who took up arms against the State and against whom many people held animosities in the country.

There was a need to sign the peace agreement before the armed opposition could return to Juba for implementation of the reunification. In order to break the fear factor, General James Hoth Mai, former Chief of General Staff of the SPLA, put it upon himself to convince FDs to return to Juba. It was a difficult undertaking. However, FDs relented briefly and sent their first team to Juba in June 2015 led by former Cabinet Affairs Minister Deng Alor Kuol. They were accompanied to Juba by then Vice President of South Africa H.E Cyril Ramaphosa, Secretary General of CCM, H.E Ambassador Abdurrahman Omari Kinana of Tanzania and foreign security personnel to protect the South Sudanese FDs from danger that could befall them in Juba.

Within one day, the Vice President of South Africa was puzzled by the fact that the FDs were moving freely in Juba without foreign security escort and were accorded festive parties in the homes of relatives and senior members of the SPLM/A and government. Indeed, the Vice President of South Africa declared that there was no need for the presence of foreign protection agents, and they were sent back to their countries. When the FDs' team returned to Nairobi, they reported back to their colleagues the positive development which transpired in Juba.

But, there was one dreadful conundrum in the implementation of the Arusha Agreement on the side of FDs. Pa'gan Amum made it a condition that he could only return to Juba if he was reinstated as Secretary General of the SPLM. In fact, the Arusha Agreement stipulated that those leaders that were dismissed during the political crisis of December 2013 were to be reinstated into their previous positions in the party. It was within his rights to demand such as per the articles of the Arusha Agreement.

The demand of Pa'gan Amum was not accepted by Chairman of the SPLM, Salva Kiir Mayardit. General James Hoth Mai and I met with FDs again at their residence in Windsor Hotel in Nairobi several times in an effort to persuade them to return to Juba for the reunification of the SPLM. Pa'gan Amum would say, 'I lead a group in the same way that Salva Kiir and Riek Machar lead their groups. Dr. Machar is reinstated as First Vice President, why should I not be reinstated in my previous position?'

General James Hoth went back to the Chairman of SPLM President Salva Kiir to persuade him to reinstate Pa'gan Amum as Secretary General of the SPLM. Finally, the President said, 'James, I cannot have a Secretary General who lives in Diaspora. When I see Pa'gan Amum in Juba, I will see what I can do.' This statement from the Chairman of the SPLM was telling. General James reported this to Pa'gan Amum and his group.

The former Secretary General Pa'gan Amum was encouraged by this gesture from the Chairman of the SPLM. He decided to travel to Juba with some of his colleagues on June 23, 2015 and on the same day, he was sworn in as Secretary General of the SPLM. We all breathed a sigh of relief with the hope that finally peace might have come to the country.

When Pa'gan Amum returned to Nairobi with his colleagues, they actively participated in a meeting between Dr. Machar and President Salva Kiir which was organized by President Uhuru Kenyatta of Kenya to break the deadlock on IGAD peace talks. President Uhuru was impressed by the success of Arusha process which was attributed to direct face-to-face talks between the South Sudanese belligerents. He wanted to bridge the gap between Kiir and Dr. Machar on IGAD issues which were the position of First Vice President for Riek Machar, compensation for those who were killed in Juba; transitional justice; and 53% positions allocated to SPLM/A-IO in Greater Upper Nile states' governments.

There was confusion about the outcome of this meeting. First, the meeting was largely attended by President Kiir who now utilized FDs in doing the paper-work for him. This was because Pa'gan Amum was now the Secretary General of the SPLM and those of Deng Alor and John Luk were of assistance to the President in drafting his documents.

General James Hoth Mai, Maj. Gen. Mach Paul and I were present in Nairobi Intercontinental Hotel where the President was accommodated and where deals were being made. However, we were not directly involved in the meetings of the President with President Uhuru and Dr. Riek Machar. We were made to believe by those who attended the meetings that President

Kiir agreed to all the proposed issues on the IGAD documents which were the sticking points for discussion. President Kiir's alleged consensual comments were given to President Uhuru on the same day.

However, some SPLM/A-IO members such as General Taban Deng Gai, Ambassador Ezekiel Lol Gatkuoth and Moulana Peter Gatkuoth Kor told us while this process was going on that President Kiir rejected the proposal and that was why Dr. Riek Machar asked for more time to prepare and later presented a 101-page-long document. President Uhuru asked the principals to only comment on the sticking issues and not on what was already agreed in Addis-Ababa. Dr. Riek Machar's comments encompassed points which were already agreed at the IGAD platform.

We were all flabbergasted by this long document which Dr. Machar presented. In the end, the meeting of the principals in Nairobi turned out to be an exercise in futility. Dr. Riek Machar remained in Nairobi and President Kiir returned to Juba without any meaningful announcement for the people of South Sudan who were hoping for a break-through before the Independence Day celebration on July 9, 2015.

The next IGAD meeting was set for August 5, 2015. It was anticipated that peace would be signed on that day. This round of peace talks coincided with the visit of the US President Barack Obama to Kenya on July 24, 2015. After his State visit to Kenya, President Obama went directly to Africa Union head-quarters in Addis-Ababa where he addressed African leaders. While in Addis-Ababa, he made it clear that the South Sudan Peace must be signed on August 17, 2015.

Indeed, the parties converged in the Ethiopian Capital

to sign the Agreement on the Resolution of Conflict in the Republic of South Sudan (ARCSS) on that date. All signed, but the President of South Sudan. Pa'gan Amum also signed on behalf of SPLM-FDs though he was the Secretary General of the SPLM.

This action confused everyone in the SPLM and the Government of South Sudan as Pa'gan Amum legally derelicted his duty as party Secretary General by signing an Agreement which his chairman refused to sign. It was argued that he couldn't have signed on behalf of another party (FDs) since he declared on June 23, 2015 when he took oath that, 'There was no more FDs as they now merged with the SPLM.' However, Pa'gan Amum contended that his group wanted him to sign the agreement because he was still their leader. He had no choice, but to sign on their behalf.

After this action, Pa'gan Amum decided not to return to South Sudan. He remained in exile making it difficult to implement the Arusha Declaration. Even after the President signed the ARCSS in Juba on August 26, 2015 and SPLM-IO and FDs representatives were appointed in the Transitional Government of National Unity (TGoNU) on April 28, 2016, Pa'gan Amum refused to return to South Sudan putting his commitment to peace in question. Afterwards, it became clear that FDs had actually split into two groups as one was led by Deng Alor Kuol and the other by Pa'gan Amum and this became clearer after the Revitalized Agreement was signed. The wing that is led by Deng Alor is now in the Revitalized Transitional Government of National Unity (R-TGoNU).

The other wing led by Pa'gan Amum does not recognize the Revitalized Agreement. He established a new party called

'Real SPLM' which joined with other non-signatories to the R-ARCSS to form South Sudan Opposition Movements' Alliance (SSOMA). The group is now in talks with R-TGoNU facilitated by the community of Saint' Edigio in Rome to join the peace process in South Sudan.

5.1.3.1. The SPLM Extraordinary Convention of January 7-9, 2016

As events were unfolding in the peace process, the deadline for registration of political parties in South Sudan was approaching fast. The SPLM came under intense pressure to meet the deadline for registration. But, it could not be registered without its basic documents (constitution and manifesto) debated and endorsed by the SPLM National Convention. It would be recalled that the documents were already discussed and endorsed by the National Liberation Council (NLC) on December 14-15, 2013, but the Convention didn't endorse them because of the outbreak of war in the country.

The SPLM decided to present the same documents to the SPLM National Convention for deliberation. The SPLM Extraordinary Convention was scheduled to take place, again, in the second week of December 2015, however; wise minds did not agree with this timing because December reminded people of what happened in 2013. It was postponed and rescheduled for January 7-9, 2016.

As a member of the SPLM National Convention, I attended the meeting. All the issues addressed in the Arusha Declaration were incorporated into the SPLM Constitution in the spirit of reunification. The SPLM invited members of SPLM-IO and

SPLM-FDs to take part in the discussion of documents as they were all in Juba at that time. The two groups refused to participate stating that their priority was the implementation of the IGAD brokered peace and not the reunification of the SPLM.

The guarantors of the Arusha Declaration, in the persons of Vice President H.E Cyril Ramaphosa of ANC and Ambassador Kinana of CCM, attended the convention and also tried to persuade the two SPLM splinter groups to participate. Even with this pressure from the guarantors, they did not budge. They only agreed to send their representatives to the opening and conclusion of the convention. In fact, Taban Deng of SPLM-IO and Deng Alor of FDs made remarks at the conclusion of the convention. All the basic documents of the SPLM were approved and its registration was completed in accordance with the requirements of the South Sudan Political Parties Act.

The question which continues to loom is, 'Will the SPLM factions ever unite with the mother SPLM?' The implementation of the Arusha document became unnerving. FDs have one group in government led by Deng Alor and another outside the country led by their group leader Pa'gan Amum campaigning for regime change in the international community. The guarantors became busy with their own internal political issues. Tanzania's CCM was engaged with its election of new leadership whereas South Africa's ANC was reeling with the impeachment proceedings labeled against their party leader President Jacob Zuma. That power struggle within the ANC ultimately led to the ousting of President Jacob Zuma and the election of H.E Cyril Ramaphosa as President of ANC and the country.

As a result of this political vacuum, Uganda stepped up

to the plate to assist with bridging the gap left by the Arusha partners. Some meetings of technical committees took place in Uganda by SPLM, SPLM-FDs and SPLM-IO Taban Deng group. The SPLM-IO led by Dr. Riek Machar did not attend the meetings because their chairman refused to appoint representatives to the talks. He insisted that he must first be released from house detention in South Africa as he wanted to participate in the talks in person.

Dr. Riek Machar went for medical treatment in South Africa after that exhaustive march from Juba to DRC in July 2016 after the J-1 incident where he was extracted by United Nations Stabilization Mission (MONUSCO) in that country. He was ultimately taken to Khartoum allegedly for medical treatment. While in Khartoum, he declared war against the Government of South Sudan in contravention to the conditions of his stay in Sudan. Some countries in the region and international community were convinced that the man was predisposed to violence. They decided to put him under house arrest in South Africa in October 2017 and asked the government there to enforce it. It was for that reason that he called for his release first before he could talk about the reunification of the SPLM.

As a confidence building measure, Egypt and Uganda organized another meeting between senior members of SPLM and FDs which resulted in the Cairo Declaration of November 16, 2017. This meeting reaffirmed the parties' commitment to Arusha Declaration and their desire to implement it fully through the work of the technical committees which were set up and continued to meet in Uganda.

When we met the CCM Secretary General Ambassador Kinana and ANC's National Executive Sub-Committee's member on external relations Professor Iqbal Jhazbhay at the sidelines of the Chinese Communist Party (CPC)-African Political Parties Theoretical Seminar in Beijing on November 28, 2017, the two expressed that they expected the SPLM to invite them to help with the implementation of the Arusha Declaration.

Their absence was not only that they were busy internally as we had thought, but rather that they did not want to be seen as imposing themselves to assist the SPLM groups in the implementation of the Arusha Declaration. This statement clearly indicated that there was a breakdown of communication. The SPLM assumed that since they were the guarantors, they were expected to push the parties to implement the declaration. Faced with this reality, we reported their sentiments to the leadership of the SPLM for action.

Finally, the SPLM IO-Taban Deng joined the SPLM on May 3, 2018. The FDs were considered to have joined the SPLM on May 22, 2019 on the day they attended a joint SPLM Political Bureau meeting in Juba chaired by Cde. Salva Kiir Mayardit. The leaders of the two SPLM groups have been attending SPLM Political Bureau meetings ever since.

Cde. Pa'gan Amum and a few of his other colleagues decided not to join the SPLM. Instead, they decided to form another party called 'Real SPLM' which is abbreviated as SPLM-R. It is widely speculated that SPLM-IO faction led by Dr. Riek Machar might form their own party eventually. However, there were voices which indicated that Dr. Riek Machar might decide to join the SPLM, and majority of his group might remain in the SPLM-IO. Only time would tell what the future holds for the SPLM splinter groups vis-à-vis the mother SPLM.

5.1.4. The Agreement on the Resolution of Conflict in the Republic of South Sudan (ARCSS)

The South Sudan Peace Agreement was set to be inked by March 5, 2015, but the two sides hit a deadlock. This stasis made the parties to the conflict harden their positions and cast doubt on the future of the talks. South Sudanese people and the international community were shocked by the intransigence of their leaders refusing to sign an agreement even as their people were suffering. As a result, IGAD exerted maximum pressure on the parties to sign the peace agreement or face consequences.

IGAD was also pressured by the Africa Union, the European Union, the United Nations, and Troika countries to do everything possible to make the parties sign the agreement. The failure of the South Sudanese leadership in the government and rebel movement to put the interest of the country first annoyed the Troika (US, UK and Norway). The world was quick to put the blame on Troika partners that they midwifed South Sudan into independence and yet, allowed inexperienced and self-serving South Sudanese leaders to drag the young country to war with impunity.

In fact, the Government of Sudan was the most amused as their political mantra was proven true that South Sudanese can not govern themselves as they are divided by tribalism and that the only glue which held them together was their fight against the north. It is the Government of Sudan which has been keeping peace among them. According to them, "If the Government of Sudan is no longer there, they will not be able to govern themselves" (Deng, 2018, p. 35).

Since the parties to the conflict refused to sign for peace,

United States proposed sanctions against individual Generals in the SPLM/A-IO and in the Government of South Sudan that they deemed to have obstructed peace. Six generals on both sides were put on the list of sanctions. On the side of the government, Lt. General Gabriel Jok Riak (Commander of Sector I), Maj. General Marial Chinoung Yol (Commander of Tiger Brigade) and Maj. General Santino Deng Wol (Commander of Division III). The SPLM/A-IO list was composed of Maj. General Simon Gatwech Dual (Chief of Staff), Maj. General James Koang Chol (Commander of Special Divison One) and Maj. General Peter Gatdeet Yak, (Deputy Chief of Staff for Operations).

Additional threats of sanctions were uttered against unknown senior people in the government and rebel movement. However, both the government and the rebels did not budge to the international threats. When South Sudan peace agreement could not be signed in March, IGAD indicated that they were searching for a rejuvenated strategy to kick start the peace talks once again.

IGAD added other countries to their group which came to be known as IGAD-Plus. The new group now included representatives of IGAD (Djibouti, Ethiopia, Kenya, Somalia, Sudan, Uganda); representatives of AU 5 (Algeria, Chad, Nigeria, Rwanda, South Africa); the African Union Commission; the People's Republic of China; the European Union; the Co-Chair of IGAD Partners Forum; and the Troika (Kingdom of Norway, United Kingdom, and the United States of America).

The group drafted for South Sudan what they called 'Agreement on the Resolution of Conflict in the Republic of South Sudan' (ARCSS). They invited both the government and rebel negotiating teams to Addis-Ababa to take this draft to their principals for consultations. As it turned out, in the next round of meetings in Addis-Ababa where IGAD Heads of State and Governments were present, there was no room for negotiation on the draft. It was a take it or leave it approach with tough consequences for intransigence by IGAD-Plus. President Obama was said to have told the leadership of the African Union when he was in Addis-Ababa that he wanted the peace agreement to be signed by August 17, 2015. The IGAD and AU were racing against such deadline.

As the August 17, 2015 deadline approached, it was clear that Dr. Riek Machar and Pa'gan Amum were going to sign the document. President Salva Kiir was adamantly opposed to the text of the document as it contained clauses which infringed on the security and sovereignty of South Sudan. As expected, Dr. Riek Machar and Pa'gan Amum signed the document along with numerous civil society groups and other witnesses who attended the talks on August 17, 2015.

President Salva Kiir asked for more time to consult with his government and the people of South Sudan. He returned to Juba and conducted consultations. In Juba, people divided themselves into two groups. There were those opposed to the agreement, and these were the majority of the close allies of the President. This group comprised mostly of members of the negotiating team in Addis-Ababa.

The other was a pro-peace group. This group believed that the people have suffered enough, and that South Sudan had lost allies in the international community. Moreover, the rebellion was spreading across the country. It was no longer limited to Upper Nile Region. There was no choice, but to save the country from destruction. Despite the inadequacies of ARCSS, they said it was better than a good war. They urged the President to sign the agreement.

President Salva Kiir did something that only those who know him closely would get their heads around. He decided to please both camps by writing 'reservations' to the agreement in order to please those opposed to peace. He also signed the peace agreement for those who wanted peace on August 26, 2015 in Freedom Hall in Juba at 5:02pm. The signature came as a big surprise to those who opposed peace because they believed that President Kiir was not going to sign. Foreign dignitaries including then Prime Minister Haile Mariam Dessaleign of Ethiopia who also doubled as Chairman of IGAD, President Museveni of Uganda, Deputy President of South Africa, and Vice President of Sudan, among others, witnessed the signing of the Agreement in the Freedom Hall in Juba.

5.1.5. Setbacks to the Implementation of ARCSS

The presence of two groups in the Government of President Salva Kiir was an open secret. One group supported ARCSS as it would stop bloodshed in the country. The other was searching for a better deal which may have suited the interest of the government.

When the President formed committees for implementation of the agreement, most of those opposed to the agreement headed them. This mismatch clutched the process of implementation. As a result, the arrival of the opposition's advance team to Juba was delayed due to lack of interest on the part of those in charge of the reception.

Another test to the agreement was the security arrangement mechanism which was discussed in Addis–Ababa. While the government readily signed the minutes of the security arrangement along with former detainees, the SPLM/A–IO did not sign because their leader Dr. Riek Machar needed more forces in Juba for their protection. This was contrary to the provision of the agreement and that represented a stumbling block to the implementation of the agreement.

When both Dr. Riek Machar and Vice President James Wani Igga went to New York for the United Nations General Assembly meeting in September 2015, at the request of the UN Secretary General Ban Ki-moon, they sought to meet US Security Advisor Susan Rice. Rice turned down their meeting request stating that the leaders of South Sudan were not serious about peace implementation. This was because Dr. Machar refused to sign the minutes of the security arrangement and President Kiir, while Wani Igga was in America, issued a Presidential Order creating 28 states for South Sudan on October 20, 2015.

The creation of new states was widely perceived by international community as a violation of the peace agreement which was signed on the basis of the ten states of South Sudan. It was John Kerry, former US Secretary of State, who carried the day by meeting the two mortified leaders of South Sudan. Kerry told them that their decisions to refuse to sign the minutes of the security arrangement and creation of more states were counterproductive to the peace process in the country and therefore, the US administration was disappointed by these actions.

The message from the international community was so stern that it forced Dr. Machar to sign the minutes of the security arrangement when he returned to Addis-Ababa. President Kiir was forced to initiate a constitutional amendment process for the creation of 28 states through the National Legislative Assembly. Initially, the Presidential Order 36/2015, stated that it was neither negotiable nor subject to discussion. However, due to international pressure, the President had to allow the parliamentary process to take its natural course.

The President was supposed to appoint governors for new states within 30 working days from the date of the Order. Nonetheless, by initiating a constitutional amendment process, the President had given the power to the National Assembly and Council of States to carry out their duty before anything else could be done.

The Assembly received the amendment from the Minister of Justice on November 18, 2015. The amendment Bill was submitted to the Assembly's Justice and Legislation Committee which reported to August House after 30 days as required by law.

The Justice Committee in the Assembly amended Article 162 (1) of the Transitional Constitution of the Republic of South Sudan, 2011 which limited the number of states in South Sudan to ten and gave President Salva Kiir the right to establish any number of states in the country. Furthermore, Articles 164 and 165 which stated that Members of state Legislative Assemblies and governors of states must be elected respectively were amended in order to give the President the power to appoint them.

Then the proposed amendment document was passed on to Council of States for deliberations. The Council did not take long to amend the Constitution and passed the Bill to President for assent. Thereafter, the President dissolved ten states and appointed governors for 28 states on December 24, 2015 and I was appointed as Governor of Latjor state.

The Creation of 28 states became a divisive factor in South Sudan politics. On the one hand, the proponents of 28 states articulated that this was a demand by the people of South Sudan who petitioned the President for more states. In fact, the Murle people of Jonglei state fought against the Government of South Sudan in 2010 partly because they needed to have their own state. Lou Nuer of the same state also demanded to have their state. There were people in Equatoria who requested to have more states. In Greater Bahr El Ghazal, voices were heard for the same issue. Indeed, as the President argued, this was not only a popular demand of the people, but part of the SPLM policy of 'taking towns to the people.'

The opponents of this idea postulated that creation of more states would undermine the signed peace agreement as the SPLM-IO would not be supportive of 28 states as their 21 state proposal was rejected by the government during the negotiations in Addis-Ababa. Rejection of 28 states by SPLM-IO would mean that peace would not be achieved, and war would continue.

They further expressed that South Sudan was divided into 28 states along ethnic lines which was deemed to threaten national cohesion and unity. This was true in the case of states where the Nuer were the majority. The Nuer were allocated their own exclusive states. All ethnic minorities that used to live with the Nuer in the same states were taken into other states even when they didn't have borders with them.

For example, the Dinka of Pigi county in Jonglei who lived

in the vicinity of Fangak state were administratively taken to Eastern Nile state as were the Komo people from Latjor to the same state. A similar situation also happened in Unity state where the Dinka of Abiemnhom and Pariang, who do not have border with each other were united to form Ruweng state while Mayom county of Bul Nuer, who are in their midst, was united with other Nuer counties to form Northern Liech state.

The third sentiment was related to economic viability of the new states. Some of the newly created states used to be one county and their economic viability was questioned by many analysts. Furthermore, South Sudan was under economic pressure due to the civil war. The economy became so dissolute that salaries for civil servants could not be paid on time. In addition, development of new state capitals would be daunting given the economic status of the country. The question was that if the economy could not support ten states, how could it now support 28 states? This became practically true during the implementation phase as most states could not support their headquarters due to conflict and lack of resources.

These two dichotomous views brought about the split in the government circles between the progenitors of 28 states and those opposed to the idea. As a matter of fact, when the Bill to amend the Transitional Constitution to allow for the creation of 28 states was taken to the Assembly for deliberations, 28 members of Parliament from the Nuer and Equatoria SPLM membership boycotted the sitting in protest.

However, the Bill was passed and the SPLM leadership of the Assembly devised a strategy to punish its MPs who boycotted the sitting. They removed them from positions of Chairpersons of Specialized Committees in the Assembly by taking away their perks. Some members of parliament were subjected to investigation by members of the SPLM Political Bureau and National Liberation Council as to why they boycotted the sitting.

Although these MPs were pardoned in the end by the SPLM leadership, the investigation sparked a lot of animosity and anger among MPs. As a result, Gatwech Lam Puoch from Nasir county, Upper Nile state, Pasquale Clement Batali of Najero, Justin Joseph Marona of Maridi constituencies in Western Equatorial state as well as Martin Mabil Kong of Rubkona, Unity state defected to SPLM/A-IO of Riek Machar in October 2016 in protest of what they viewed as the violation of the right of MPs to express their views freely and vote conscientiously.

CHAPTER SIX

The Transitional Government of National Unity (TGoNU)

AFTER THE SIGNATURE OF ARCSS, the parties to the agreement embarked on the implementation process. It would take three Transitional Governments of National Unity which are designated here for clarity as TGoNU, TGoNU II and TGoNU III to bring relative peace to the country as the parties were not committed to the peaceful implementation of the agreement. This analysis begins with the establishment of TGoNU.

Since the arrival of the advance team from SPLM/A-IO to Juba on December 21, 2015, the return of Dr. Riek Machar to Juba was an uphill battle. First, there was too much suspicion that if Dr. Riek Machar returned to Juba, there could be military confrontation again since he would have his police and military forces as stipulated in the Agreement. The issue of two separate armies during the interim period was a controversial matter as it was a surefire recipe for armed confrontation. However, western governments were consistently in favour of the two armies as demanded by the opposition.

In order to expedite the return of SPLM/A-IO to Juba, President Salva Kiir appointed David Deng Athorbei, then Minister of Finance and Economic Planning, to lead the reception committee. It was only then that the SPLM/A-IO's first team landed in Juba on December 21, 2015. As a result, Dr. Riek Machar arrived in Juba on April 26, 2016 and was sworn into the Office of the First Vice President on the same day.

Dr. Riek Machar was given a residence at Jabel area near UNMISS base. This was the area where the majority of his forces were assembled prior to his arrival in Juba. On April 28, 2016, the Transitional Government of National Unity (TGoNU) was formed. Since this government was composed of different political parties, it was hoped that it would bring peace and stability in the country.

However, contrary to the expectations, that government was awashed with enigmas. There were sticky issues in the agreement which were to be unpacked and implemented. One of them was the leadership of the Transitional National Legislative Assembly (TNLA). According to the agreement, this post would go to the people of Greater Equatoria Region. They were the aggrieved party since Dr. James Wani Igga, who deputized Salva Kiir in the government during the crisis, was obliged to vacate his post for Riek Machar. Now the question was whether the Speaker of the Assembly would come from SPLM-IO or SPLM from Equatoria.

The common understanding was that it was the SPLM which lost its position to Dr. Riek Machar. Therefore, the leadership of the Assembly was for SPLM members from Equatoria. When that fact was established, the procedure to install the leader of the Assembly became another dreadful conundrum. The text of the agreement stated that the leader of the Assembly would be selected. The word 'selected' became a source of confusion in the Transitional National Legislative Assembly. 'Selected' to SPLM leadership meant that the SPLM caucus would select a cadre from Equatoria who would afterwards be endorsed by all members of the Assembly. However, to the SPLM-IO, it meant "election" by the whole Assembly of whoever they wanted among the SPLM members from Equatoria Region. This became so contentious an issue that it delayed the recon-stitution of the leadership of the Assembly. The SPLM was not convinced that all its members in the caucus would vote for its candidate because it was clear that some SPLM members in the Assembly were sympathetic to SPLM-IO position.

On June 10, 2016, I went to Nairobi for personal reasons, but Vice President Dr. James Wani directed his protocol officer to look for me as he was planning a trip to Addis-Ababa to speak to South Sudanese who lived there about the implemen-tation of the peace agreement. I was instructed to go to Addis-Ababa on June 17, 2016 to meet with Dr. James Wani there. I went as instructed and met with the Vice President at Bole International Airport.

In the next day, the Vice President made his presentation to South Sudanese in the Civil Service University Auditorium in Addis-Ababa. Before our return to South Sudan, we met with then Ethiopian Minister of Foreign Affairs, Dr. Theodros Adhanom. One of the topics Vice President Dr. James Wani discussed with the Minister pertained to the method of installing the leadership of the TNLA in South Sudan.

As usual, Dr. James Wani put the issue comically to the Ethiopian Foreign Minister, 'We understand that your ambassador was the one who wrote this section on the agreement. He used the phrase 'to select' the head of the Assembly. What did he mean by selection?'

Dr. Adhanom was not devoid of comedy himself, 'Well, your government delegation dismissed our ambassador during the talks accusing him of taking side during the negotiations. So, I don't know if he would agree to help you understand his phrase 'to select.' However, we will try to beg him to help all of us understand it.' The Foreign Minister promised us to get a written response from the said Ambassador soon which he would then transmit to South Sudan.

This was the extent to which the agreement was scrutinized by both sides to the conflict in South Sudan to the point where reading between the lines was compulsory. However, before the explanation could come, the war broke out again in J-1 Presidential Palace on July 8, 2016.

There were also other issues which hindered the implementation of the agreement such as the selection of cantonment sites for opposition forces, establishment of 28 states and so forth.

6.1. The J-1 Incident of July 8, 2016

While wrangling among politicians continued in the halls of government unabated, military and security complications surfaced on the streets of Juba. The security situation in Juba deteriorated as the two armies crossed each other on the roads which resulted in the death of personnel. On July 2, 2016, Colonel George Gismala from SPLA-IO was killed in a little restaurant in Kator community. He was allegedly killed by SPLA and National Security agents. On the same day, Lt. Domach Koat Pinyin was also shot dead in Jabel community. This act was again attributed to armed agents of the Government of South Sudan.

On July 5, 2016, a tinted vehicle carrying members of SPLM/A-IO was stopped by government security forces for inspection on Gudele road near Lou Clinic. In this search, the SPLA and national security agents took two guns from the vehicle. The SPLM/A-IO personnel were upset by this as they viewed it as an act of humiliation.

On July 7, 2016, the SPLM/A-IO forces came up to Gudele area near Lou Clinic and demanded the return of their guns from SPLA and National Security personnel. This resulted in altercation after which the SPLM/A-IO personnel opened fire killing five and wounding two of the government personnel. Accused as responsible for this incident in the SPLM/A-IO vehicle, were Col. David Riew and Captain Gatluak Thian Deng both of whom were bodyguards of Dr. Riek Machar.

These military incidents made the political and security atmosphere in Juba very tense. As a result, it behooved both President Salva Kiir and First Vice President Dr. Riek Machar to form a committee to investigate the causes of these incidents and to come up with the report within seven days.

The President called for security meeting in the State House popularly known as J-1 to discuss these security issues and how to resolve them with First Vice President Dr. Machar, Vice President Dr. James Wani Igga and other senior government officials concerned with security file. This meeting was scheduled for Friday July 8, 2016. As a result, the regular Council of Ministers' meeting which took place on Fridays was cancelled as security took precedence. According to the President, he cancelled the meeting of the Council of Ministers because he was aware of a plan to kill government officials in the meeting that Friday by SPLM/A-IO security forces.

First Vice President Dr. Riek Machar, as usual came, with a convoy of guards from his base in Jabel. The meeting started in J-1 with all the principals present. I left my state coordination office in Gudele at about 4:00pm and passed behind J-1 to my residence which was one block down the road. I was concerned about what I saw behind J-1. I made a comment to my personnel in the vehicle that the way the soldiers stood adjacent to each other holding their guns at 45-degree angle was dangerous. I even joked that if someone stumbles on any object that makes noise now, those soldiers would start shooting at each other. Sure enough, at about 5:20pm, gun fight started in J-1.

The initiator of this fight was as mysterious as the initiator of December 15, 2013 crisis. Who did start the skirmishes in J-1? Both government and SPLM/A-IO circles around the world provided different versions as usual about what happened. Either side tried to blame the incident on the other and presented itself as a victim.

The spokesman of Dr. Riek Machar James Gatdeet Dak who lived in Nairobi at the time put out a statement on his Facebook page to alert all SPLM/A-IO members that Dr. Riek Machar was arrested in J-1 meeting. This was around 4:30pm. This Facebook message caused a lot of commotion among SPLM/A-IO circles trying to verify the authenticity of the report. In fact, the report was false. Dr. Machar had not been arrested. People wondered up to this time as to what was the intention of James Gatdeet Dak in posting such a dangerous and false message. Did someone intentionally misinform James Gatdeet that Dr. Riek Machar was arrested and what could have been the motive? What was that information supposed to achieved? He is the only one to answer those questions.

Just before 5:00pm, James Gatdeet Dak, for whatever reason, removed the information from his Facebook page. Immediately, he was called on it by many government supporters including Ambassador Gordon Buay in United States, who forced him to restore the statement on his page. James Gatdeet did not deny putting out the statement. In fact, he restored the statement and left it on his page laying it bare for all to see. Subsequently, this statement was considered as the first trigger of J-1 incident as shall be presented later.

However, according to government account given by Minister of Information, Michael Makuei Lueth and later corroborated by Presidential spokesman Ateny Wek Ateny, some SPLM/A-IO soldiers left their base in Jabel with 72 textures (Toyota pick-ups) loaded with fighters commanded by Lt. Col. David Riew and Captain Gatluak Thian. They also reported that one of the vehicles was an ambulance full of weapons and ammunitions. When these soldiers arrived in the vicinity of J-1, they tried to enter by force to rescue Dr. Riek Machar who was reported to have been arrested by President Salva Kiir.

During the altercation at the gate of J-1 between Lt. Col. David

Riew and President Kiir's bodyguard, who happened to be a Nuer from Bentiu. The former fired his gun and killed the latter.

Immediately, another Presidential bodyguard member shot dead Lt. Col. David Riew. As the battle ensued, Captain Gatluak Thian was also killed. The fight took place outside and inside the premises of J-1. Bullet holes on the fence and offices at J-1 were clear evidence of a dog fight which continued until a stormy rain came from nowhere and seemed to have stopped it.

The government also reported that when Dr. Riek Machar went to J-1 meeting, he carried a pistol on his person. That pistol was allegedly removed by Minister of National Security Gen. Isaac Obuto Mamur Mete before he entered the Office of the President where the meeting was to be held. According to these government officials, Dr. Riek Machar's aim was to kill President Kiir so that he could take over the position of the President. In other words, Dr. Riek Machar went to J-1 meeting with the intention to kill President Salva Kiir and take over the government.

As the fight subsided, President Salva Kiir, First Vice President Dr. Riek Machar and Vice President Dr. James Wani Igga, gave a live press conference in J-1 telling the people of South Sudan to remain calm as they stated, 'We do not know what caused this fighting in the State House.' This clearly indicated that all of them did not really know what happened until they returned to their bases for information on the cause of the incident.

Now, President Salva Kiir had the burden of taking Dr. Riek Machar to his residence in Jabel area. According to the President, he called the UN Special Representative of the Secretary General and Head of UNMISS in South Sudan H.E Ellen Margrethe Løj to take him, but she was already hiding in the US Embassy in Juba and therefore said that she could not help. Then the President called the

Deputy Special Representative of the UN Secretary General who reported that he was also hiding in the Embassy of the European Union.

Apparently, those whose mission was to protect the people and provide security for South Sudanese were in hiding. So, Salva Kiir had to do this himself. He saw that all the vehicles of Dr. Riek Machar were damaged in the parking lot during the fighting.

The President sent his guards to his house and bring his bullet proof private car to the office. When the car came, he took Dr. Riek Machar personally to the car and opened the door of the car for him. Then, he ordered Gen. Akol Koor, Director General for Internal Security Bureau and Gen. Marial Chinoung Yol, Commander of the Republican Guards (Tiger Brigade), to escort him to his home at Jabel. The President told Dr. Machar to call him to confirm his safe arrival at home.

When Dr. Machar reached his residence, he called the President and thanked him for his help. This was how Dr. Riek Machar got out from J-1. The same narration was repeated by President Kiir to us when we met him as senior Nuer SPLM leadership on July 19, 2016 in J-1. The meeting was for a different purpose, but he took the liberty to tell us what happened and what he did to save Dr. Riek Machar.

The SPLM/A-IO group rejected this government account and advanced a different theory on the events of July 8. According to their sources, Dr. Riek Machar was lured into J-1 not because there was a meeting, but rather because there was a plan to kill him there.

They reported that the SPLA and the national security personnel fired the first bullet to kill Dr. Machar's bodyguards so that they could kill their leader afterwards. Their narrative purported that Dr. Machar's bodyguards overpowered the SPLA, National Security agents and Presidential Protection to the point where they had to willingly spare the life of President Salva Kiir in J-1.

The SPLM/A-IO narrative also denied that there was any rein-forcement under the command of Lt. Col. David Riew and Capt. Gatluak Thian sent from Jabel to rescue Dr. Riek Machar. The SPLM/A-IO group accused some elements within their ranks and certain individuals in the government for planning to get rid of Dr. Riek Machar and President Salva Kiir together so that they could take over the power from these two leaders.

I was intimately familiar with the story of the ambulance. The ambulance was going to pick up the body of late Lt. Col. Samahan Koang Kueth (Koang Nyalual Diew Gai) who was an officer from SPLA shell five (batch five). He passed away in the home of his uncle John Kor Diew in Hay Referendum due to natural causes. Inside the ambulance were Jock Diw Gai, his son Chan and their Dinka driver. The ambulance belonged to Dar Petroleum Operating Company (D-POC) Ltd. where Jock Diw Gai worked. The administration of the company gave him the ambulance to take the body of his relative to the mortuary at the SPLA Military Hospital in Giyada.

The ambulance was driven from Quality Hotel where Jock Diu Gai lived. Unfortunately, when it arrived behind J-1, firing started. The people in the ambulance were killed instantly as it was attacked by both sides. However, the J-1 incident video which surfaced later on YouTube showed one of the victims on the ground on the driver's side holding up one hand. Most likely, that was the driver. He was still moving his hands at the time the video was shot, probably trying to call for help while soldiers were busy cleaning the area. His blood covered the place in which he laid.

It became clear from the narratives provided that neither side had any prior plan to start fighting, at least not in that meeting. This was because if Riek Machar went to J-1 to assassinate President Salva Kiir, he could have gone there with more troops than just rely on few bodyguards and a pistol which he denied possessing.

By the same token, if Salva Kiir wanted to get rid of Dr. Riek Machar, he could have killed him since majority of his guards were eliminated. He could not have bothered to take him home safely. If he did not want to kill him in his office, he could have sent him without escort or lay an ambush to eliminate him. From the evidence available, he did not have any intention to assassinate Dr. Riek Machar. I remember in our meeting with the President, someone asked him why he let Dr. Riek Machar go alive. His response was, 'I did not create Riek Machar. Only his creator will decide when to take him.' That answer amazed a lot of people. It indicated that he did not have any plan to assassinate Dr. Riek Machar.

According to both government and UN reports, the fighting in J-1 killed 150 people including 33 civilians (Sudantribune, July 9, 2016). The following morning was the Independence Day (9th of July). There was no expectation to celebrate the day because President Salva Kiir earlier cancelled the festivities due to what he termed as lack of funds to conduct the celebration. However, the reason was more than lack of funds. It was insecurity in the city as he reported to us later in another meeting.

Both the President and Dr. Riek Machar were expected to give televised and radio addresses to the nation on that day. But, due to the political and military confrontation on the other day, this could not take place. The 9th of July was exceptionally quiet. There was no fighting as some communications continued between the President and the First Vice President Dr. Riek Machar.

The SPLM/A-IO military leadership in Jabel was angered by the fact that their small force which accompanied Dr. Riek Machar was decimated in J-1 and their colleagues wanted to revenge. As a result, the military leadership of SPLM/A-IO did not take Dr. Riek Machar's advice, which did not favour the resumption of fighting.

The fighting started again on July 10, 2016 and continued up to the 11th of July when the SPLM/A-IO forces in Jabel were dislodged from their position. Heavy machine guns and helicopter gunships were utilized. UNMISS estimated that in the battles of July 10-11, 272 people were killed; unknown numbers were wounded; and more than 12, 000 people fled to UNMISS POC sites in Juba as tens of thousands more fled to the neighbouring countries as refugees.

After a number of battles in the vicinity of Juba, Dr. Riek Machar and his forces were extricated, and they started a long march: 40 days from Juba to Democratic Republic of Congo (DRC). They were pursued by government forces both by land and by air. Dr. Riek Machar became extremely exhausted from this painstaking journey, especially after the dislocation of his knee when he had to be carried by soldiers for five days. However, they managed to cross the border into the Democratic Republic of the Congo (DRC).

Dr. Machar, his wife and about ten other close associates were extracted from Garamba Forest by UN Stabilization Mission in DRC (MONUSCO) on August 17, 2016 around 5:00pm. They left the rest of their forces there extremely exhausted and almost at the verge of starvation. Had it not been the provision of food assistance by MONUSCO on August 18, 2016 under the direction of David Gresly, Deputy Special Representative of the UN Secretary General in that organization, most of the forces of Dr. Riek Machar could have died.

MONUSCO had entered into negotiation with the leadership of SPLM/A-IO to accept disarmament and be declared as non-combatants in order for them to receive international protection in accordance with international humanitarian law. It was only after this declaration that MONUSCO airlifted the rest of the so called 'former SPLM/A-IO fighters' in Garamba from August 23 to September 1, 2016. They landed in Dungu airbase where they proceeded to Bunia and Goma. However, almost all these declared non-combatants returned to the bush as fighters for Dr. Riek Machar in direct contravention to the terms of their agreement with MONUSCO.

Dr. Riek Machar was subsequently taken to Khartoum by the Government of Sudan where he underwent medical treatment. While in that country under medical grounds, he declared war against the Government of South Sudan allegedly in violation of the terms of his stay for medical care in Khartoum. His declaration of war angered a lot of his western allies and the Sudanese Government. After this, he left for further medical treatment in South Africa where he was put under house arrest by the authorities there allegedly at the request of IGAD member states and the international community. The world believed that Dr. Machar became a factor for instability and persecution of war in South Sudan in which millions of people were displaced and tens of thousands more died.

6.2. The Spill of J-1 Incident on Equatoria Region

After the crisis of 2013, Equatoria, like Bahr El Ghazal Region, remained relatively peaceful. Even though some prominent Equatorians like Alfred Lado Gore and Henry Dilla Odwar joined Dr. Machar, there was no significant fighting in Equatoria. It was only after the J-1 incident that Equatoria was engulfed in war.

After the formation of TGoNU, debates were held in the Council of Ministers regarding the establishment of cantonment sites for the fighters of SPLM/A-IO as provided for in the ARCSS. However, the Government of South Sudan insisted that these sites would only be set up in Upper Nile region where Dr. Machar had the majority of supporters. This meant that fighters in Equatoria and Bahr El Ghazal were discredited and denied the right to cantonment.

This approach did not gratify the politicians and fighters from Equatoria who had always called for the SPLA and other organized forces to be diversified and inclusive. By that they meant the army was dominated by Nuer and Dinka. They needed their fighters to be integrated into the national army and other organized forces so that they could have fair representation in this sector.

In light of this, the rebel activities were scaled up in Equatoria by blocking roads from Nimule, Yei and Kaya to Juba in order to force the TGoNU to recognize that opposition existed in Equatoria and that there was a need to establish cantonment sites for them. When the J-1 incident happened, Dr. Machar passed through Equatoria and that was their opportunity to join the rebellion in big numbers, thereby making the region the new battle ground from 2016 to 2018.

As the government pursued Dr. Machar and his forces, hundreds of thousands of Equatorians were displaced and fled to refugee camps in Uganda. Various towns and villages were razed in the wake of the new war. The destruction, human suffering and violations of human rights were documented by the United Nations Mission in South Sudan (UNMISS, 2016) and Human Rights Watch (HRW, 2016). The two organizations blamed the killing, displacement of civilians and destruction of properties on the government forces.

In reprisal, Dinka civilians who tried to flee from Yei to Juba were intercepted on the roads and were summarily executed by the rebels in Equatoria. It was during this time that the term 'MTN' was coined by some Equatoria rebels to describe Dinkas in Equatoria. MTN is a telephone network available in many different states of Equatoria. The application of such term by Equatoria rebels to describe the Dinka meant that the Dinka left their states and occupied other people's territories in Equatoria. This also meant that whoever was described as MTN was marked for execution by the rebels in this region.

The same situation of war also spilled over to Western Bahr El Ghazal state, especially in Wau and its vicinity where thousands of Fartit, Balanda and other ethnic minorities were killed and displaced by the Dinka majority (UNMISS, 2016). This struggle within the state ended up with the dismissal of Governor Elias Waya, an ethnic Fartit and his subsequent imprisonment by the Government of South Sudan.

6.3. The Shift of Alliances in the SPLM/A-IO Before and After J-1 Incident

The SPLM/A-IO was a shaky alliance of politicians and military officers with different interests. Its composition was made up of an unlikely coalition of groups and individuals some of whom have unpredictable behaviours and tendencies. The Juba incident of December 2013 forced many Nuer people to leave Juba for safety. Majority of them, who were never allies of Dr. Riek Machar, got themselves in the same bush with him. Since Riek Machar had the support of Nuer civilians in the villages, he became their *de facto* leader after their consultative meeting in Nasir in January 2014. However, this didn't mean that all the politicians and military generals (of the SPLM/A- IO) agreed with that choice.

This lack of solid unity within the SPLM/A-IO group came to a head when the majority of military generals defected and formed their own movement on August 11, 2015. Among these were General Peter Gatdeet Yak, General Gathoth Gatkuoth, General Chuol Gaka, General Tanginye and many senior politicians including Michael Mario Dhuor, Timothy Tot Chol, Gabriel Yoal Dok, Changson Lew Chang and many others. Their group came to be known as Federal Democratic Party (FDP) led by Gen. Gathoth, with its military wing, South Sudan Armed Forces (SSAF) led by Gen. Peter Gatdeet as its principal commander. Since their group was composed of the most senior military officers founding the SPLM/A-IO, it was christened, 'The Group of Generals.'

A majority of these people stated that they left Dr. Riek Machar's movement because he never listened to 'advice, lacked direction and vision.' These were poignantly the same reasons he blamed President Salva Kiir for triggering 2013 crisis. The second reason was that they accused close relatives of Dr. Machar for mistreatment of others in the movement. But, the unity of the newly formed group could not hold either due to the nature of the personalities involved and the leadership rivalry which surfaced among them.

They sub-divided into the group of General Gathoth Gatkuoth and that of General Peter Gatdeet which called itself the South Sudan Liberation Army (SSLA). The group of Gathoth Gatkuoth signed a separate Memorandum of Understanding (MOU) with the Government of South Sudan represented by Tut Gatluak Manimee on December 25, 2015. Because of the signature of the MOU, Hon. Changson Lew Chang parted ways with General Gathoth. The two groups from henceforth engaged in claim and counter claim of the name of Federal Democratic Party (FDP).

The group of Gen. Gathoth came to Juba on March 13, 2016. I was requested by one of the Directors General of National Security Service to welcome them at Juba international airport. This was because some of their members were not sure of their physical safety in Juba and since General Gathoth is from my state, I was asked to go and welcome him as his governor.

Their main agenda to come to Juba was to implement the MOU they signed with the government. However, the Government of South Sudan did not give positions to General Gathoth and his group because their positions were in the per-centage allocated to Dr. Riek Machar's SPLM/A-IO as they were the commanders who fought for him. General Gathoth was not pleased with this response, but he had to maintain a low profile because the politics of South Sudan was on a roller coaster at that time.

When the Transitional Government of National Unity was formed, General Taban Deng Gai, believed that he was going to be appointed as Minister for Petroleum, as per their earlier plan in the SPLM/A-IO. Instead, he was appointed as Minister for Mining. It was later revealed that Taban Deng was blamed by the closest circle of Dr. Machar for being too close to President Salva Kiir and his loyalty to SPLM/A-IO was questioned by that circle.

Since the time he took oath as Minister for Mining, Taban Deng leaned more towards SPLM and old friendship ties with President Salva Kiir were mended. It is important to recall that Taban Deng and President Salva Kiir were the best of buddies before he was relieved as Governor of Unity state in 2013.

In another twist of events, Taban Deng's close friend Ambassador Ezekiel Lol Gatkuoth was not given any ministerial position by Dr. Riek Machar. Instead, he was given a senior executive position in the Office of the First Vice President Dr. Riek Machar. He saw this as a demotion, if not, humiliation by Dr. Machar and his close circle. It was alleged that Dr. Riek Machar's wife, Angelina Teny, was responsible for the removal of Taban Deng's name from the Ministry of Petroleum and the relegation of Ambassador Ezekiel in favour of Dak Duop Bichok for Ministry of Petroleum. Dak Duop and Ezekiel Lol both hail from the county of Longechuk in Upper Nile state.

While SPLM/A-IO was on this confusion of divided loyalties, the J-1 episode suddenly happened. Most Ministers of the SPLM-IO were accommodated in the Crown Hotel along airport road in Juba which was very far from Jabel where Dr.

Riek Machar was and where the battle was fought. As fighting continued in Juba on July10–11, 2016 and the majority of the SPLM/A-IO group was dislodged from Juba, their Ministers, MPs, Generals and supporters remained in hotels in Juba.

Taban Deng saw that the situation was dangerous for their group. He decided to see President Kiir on Monday July 11, 2016 while the fighting was ongoing. It was reported that Akol Paul Kordit, then Chairman of the SPLM Youth League and member of the SPLM Political Bureau, took him to the President that morning. He was welcomed with an open heart by the President. Whatever the substance of their discussion was, it probably helped contain the fighting. The remnants of SPLM/A-IO who remained in hotels were not targeted.

In his own words on one Sunday morning during worship in the Nuer Presbyterian Church in Jabel, Taban Deng said, 'I blocked a falling mountain on the Nuer in Juba.' He believed that if he did not declare his allegiance to the Government of South Sudan and was in full support of peaceful implementation of the agreement, Nuer people could have been targeted once again in Juba.

6.4. The Response of the Nuer in Government After the J-1 Incident

On July 17, 2016, SPLM Nuer leadership in Juba met in Crown Hotel. The purpose of the meeting was to discuss the increased rape crimes that were allegedly committed by security forces at check points against Nuer women on their way to and from UNMISS to Juba town.

The second was the fact that even though it was contained,

some prominent Nuer leaders were targeted including Governor Gen. Peter Bol Kong of Bieh state, myself (Governor of Latjor state), General Gathoth Gatkuoth, MPs and many others. The third agenda was the fate of Gen. Gathoth Gatkuoth and his group who signed an MOU with the government and were not given any positions by government. The fourth was about what to do with the remnants of SPLM/A-IO leadership that were left in hotels in Juba.

It was our assessment that for peace to continue, this SPLM/A-IO group in Juba must appoint a Nuer leader to replace Dr. Riek Machar as the vacuum created by his departure threatened the validity of the Agreement. We agreed to meet the President and to ask him to replace Dr. Machar with the choice of the remnant members of the SPLM/A-IO in Juba.

After this meeting, I went upstairs to Taban Deng's room in the Crown Hotel and briefed him on our resolutions including that the SPLM/A-IO group needed to elect a new leader for their group in order to be relevant in Juba. That person would replace Dr. Riek Machar as First Vice President. I went to the extent of telling him that he should be the one to replace Dr. Riek Machar due to his seniority and the fact that he also hails from Nuer community. He was receptive to our resolutions and told me that he was going to call their group for a meeting to address the situation. I gathered he was already contemplating along the same lines.

These and many other points were recorded as resolutions for the meeting with President Salva Kiir on Monday July 19, 2016. I was asked to read the resolutions in our meeting with President Salva Kiir and it was broadcast in its entirety on SSBC. The President responded positively to our petition.

He appreciated the fact that we were united on this as SPLM leaders from the Nuer community to have a replacement for Dr. Riek Machar for the validity of the peace agreement.

In just a few days, the SPLM/A-IO group met in the Crown Hotel and chose General Taban Deng Gai as the Chairman and Commander-in-Chief of the SPLM/A-IO. Then, the SPLM/A-IO group wrote to President Salva Kiir asking him to appoint Taban Deng as First Vice President. This was in accordance with the provisions of the Agreement on the Resolution of Conflict in the Republic of South Sudan (ARCSS) which called for such action to take place in cases like this one. This was how General Taban Deng was appointed as First Vice President of the Republic of South Sudan.

6.5. The Transitional Government of National Unity Two (TGoNU II)

After President Salva Kiir appointed Gen. Taban Deng Gai as First Vice President of the Republic of South Sudan, there was jubilation across all political divide except those who still supported Dr. Machar. The reason for the celebration was that people knew the personal relations between Taban Deng and Salva Kiir which they believed would bring about peace in the country. Though they fell out in 2013, it was assumed that they would repair their differences and implement the agreement in the spirit of cooperation.

As expected, President Salva Kiir and First Vice President Taban Deng managed to accomplish many things in the agreement notable among them were the reconstitution of TGoNU for the second time, hence the designation TGoNU

II; reconstitution of the Transitional National Legislative Assembly (TNLA II) which stalled during the time of Dr. Riek Machar; relocation of state governments to their headquarters, especially the Nuer states, and the resolution of the impasse on 28 states.

After his appointment, Taban Deng appointed SPLM/A-IO members to the cabinet. Noteworthy was the appointment of his close friend Ambassador Ezekiel Lol Gatkuoth to the lucrative Ministry of Petroleum which Taban Deng himself wanted to occupy during the time when Dr. Riek Machar was First Vice President.

He increased the number of Nuer Ministers on the SPLM/A-IO ticket to make it commensurate with their con-tribution during the war. He went on to appoint SPLM/A-IO members to TNLA. The issue of speakership was easily resolved. The SPLM got the position of speaker while SPLM/A-IO had the deputy as stipulated in the agreement.

The matter of the 28 states became a non-issue for him as he worked very hard to address the concerns of the aggrieved communities in terms of state and county boundaries. For this reason, Central Upper Nile state was created from Eastern and Western Nile states to address the land dispute between the Chollo and Dinka Padang communities. The new states created out of this compromise were Fashoda, Central Upper Nile and Northern Upper Nile.

Maiwut state was created out of Latjor state as per the request of SPLM members from Eastern Jikany in February 2016 when they demanded four states under the leadership of community Chairman David Koak Guok. The Komo people who were included in former Eastern Nile state were returned to Maiwut state. Akobo state was carved from Bieh state as Tumbora state was from Gbudwe state. Now, South Sudan became a country with 32 states plus Abyei Special Administrative Area, there were still so many communities demanding more states. However, the President made it clear that the number of states would not exceed 36 as per his briefing to us on March 1, 2017.

The governorships of both Latjor and Maiwut states were given to SPLM/A-IO Taban. The SPLM leadership did not ask to retain one position of governor since they were in cooperative relations with Gen. Taban Deng. Even though it was reported that Gen. Taban Deng had wanted to give one governorship position to SPLM cadres as a positive gesture for inclusive relationship, the SPLM/A-IO leaders from Jikany community who were with him held grudges against SPLM cadres who were their opponents during the 2013 crisis. They got the golden opportunity to punish them politically and economically.

This arrangement effectively compromised and immobilized SPLM cadres in Latjor and Maiwut states who remained loyal and committed to the SPLM leadership and the Government of South Sudan during the crisis. Those cadres felt humiliated and abandoned by the SPLM leadership. They made this point very clearly to the Chairman of SPLM, President Salva Kiir Mayardit, in their meeting with him on March 1, 2017.

As suspected, the SPLM/A-IO governors in these two states decided to mistreat and punish those who remained loyal to the SPLM and government during the crisis of 2013 by denying their rights in the state governments. Those governors refused to use the percentage system provided for in the agreement, especially with regard to allocation of positions in the cabinets, assemblies and counties. They went to the extent of dividing the SPLM cadres politically since they controlled state resources. Cooperation between President Salva Kiir and First Vice President Taban Deng was limited to the national level as states experienced a different type of relationship between SPLM/A-IO Taban and the SPLM cadres.

When those discrepancies were brought before the leadership of the SPLM to rectify the situation, nothing was done. The leadership failed to protect its cadres from mistreatment. As a consequence, it took over nine months to form the Government of Maiwut state because of the power wrangling between SPLM and SPLM/A-IO Taban Deng's cadres in the state. This was the first time in South Sudan for such a variance of administration to happen. This power struggle continued until the dissolution of 32 states by the decision of the Presidency on February 15, 2020.

Ironically, except for Ruweng state, the governorships of Central and Northern Upper Nile, as well as Northern and Southern Liech states, were retained by the SPLM as a friendly gesture from SPLM/A-IO leader Taban Deng Gai.

6.6. The Revitalization of ARCSS

After the appointment of First Vice President for the Transitional Government of National Unity (TGoNU II) on July 23, 2016, war spread and intensified in Equatoria and Bahr El Ghazal regions. More people from these regions fled to the neighbouring countries for safety. Fighting also resumed in Upper Nile region without any cessation insight. The resumption of war in the whole country put into question the validly of the theory that ARCSS was still holding. It became clear that SPLM/A-IO of Dr. Riek Machar and other new rebel groups were not going to stop fighting unless something was done for peace to return to the country.

The IGAD countries proposed a new plan to revitalize ARCSS in order to include opposition groups that were not party to the agreement, especially to bring the group of Dr. Riek Machar to the table again. The principles for revitalization were presented by Dr. Ismael Wais, IGAD Special Envoy for South Sudan, as follows: 'To restore permanent ceasefire; resume full and inclusive implementation of the 2015 peace agreement; develop revised and realistic timelines; as well as implementation schedule towards a democratic election at the end of the transitional period.' By 'inclusivity, ' Dr. Ismael Wais opened a Pandora's box in South Sudan's political landscape. So many new and briefcase rebel groups sprang up in the country at an alarming rate demanding to be included in the power-sharing arrangement which now became the new way to access government positions and resources.

Initially, the Government of South Sudan made it very clear that a re-negotiation of ARCSS was not an option. It was rather interested to improve on the parts of the agreement which were not working well for 'revitalization' to be meaningful.

The SPLM/A-IO Taban Deng group in government was ambivalent towards the 'revitalization' initiative. They perceived it as a stratagem to throw them out and bring Dr. Riek Machar back to the government since they did not manage to silence the guns in the country. And their fear was well founded. If the example of the way they treated the committed and loyal Nuer members of the SPLM in Government, especially in Eastern

Jikany (Latjor and Maiwut states), could serve as a warning, then the writing was on the wall for them.

The SPLM leadership has recently been accused of developing a tendency to reward rebellion at the expense of committed cadres who fought and stood for it in an effort to tame the dissidents. In so doing, it made its power base thinner as loyal members saw greener pastures with the opposition. In fact, the most ardent critics of the SPLM now are its loyal members who blame the party for not engaging them in any meaningful activity. Whether it is fair judgement or not, that is the perception of most SPLM members at this particular point in time.

As the revitalization process continued in Addis-Ababa without any headway, a new phenomenon happened which turned everything around. Prime Minister Haile Mariam Dessaleign resigned from his positon as Prime Minister in Ethiopia due to domestic political pressure. The coming to power of a reformist Prime Minister Dr. Abiy Ahmed who inherited the Chair of IGAD from his predecessor, turned things around in the revitalization process. The new Prime Minister demanded a meeting with Dr. Riek Machar and President Salva Kiir Mayardit in Addis-Ababa. This would be the first face-to-face meeting of the two leaders in nearly two years since J-1 incident. His demand made it possible for Dr. Machar to be released from house arrest in South Africa and to travel to Addis-Ababa for such meeting. President Salva Kiir was ready to meet Dr. Machar as long as this could stop the escalation of war in the country.

After this important meeting, the new Ethiopian Prime Minister allowed the meeting to be continued in Khartoum and Kenya before it could be returned to Addis-Ababa for final signature. Then President of Sudan Field Marshal Omer Hassen El Beshir took this chance with enthusiasm. The Sudan saw the existence of peace in South Sudan as the only way to ensure peace and economic recovery in their country as they would play key role in the resumption of oil production in Unity state. This was because the oil arears which South Sudan owed to Sudan were almost fully paid and the Sudan government was looking to South Sudan for more economic cooperation in order to sustain their economy. The economic interest of Khartoum was clearly stated in the speech of President El Beshir during the signing of the agreement and in a subsequent cooperation document which was signed by the two Ministers of Petroleum (South Sudan and Sudan) in Khartoum.

In this regard, South Sudan government appointed Hon. Tut Gatluak Manimee, Presidential Advisor on Security, to lead the government negotiation team in Khartoum. His appointment had a positive impact on the progress of the peace talks. The Khartoum round of IGAD revitalization talks resulted in the Khartoum Declaration for Peace (KDP) which was signed on June 27, 2018. The parties continued to negotiate until the final Revitalized Agreement on the Resolution of conflict in the Republic of South Sudan (R-ARCSS) was signed in Addis-Ababa on September 12, 2018. The signature of this agreement ushered in a new era of hope for peace in South Sudan.

However, some members of the opposition groups did not sign the revitalized agreement stating that it didn't address the roots of the conflict in the country as they perceived them. These included National Salvation Front (NAS) of Gen. Thomas Cirilo, Gen. Paul Malong Awan's South Sudan United Front/Army (SSUF/A), Real SPLM (SPLM-R) of

Pa'gan Amum, among others. It took another initiative by the Community of Sant'Egidio in Rome (Italy) to facilitate discussions between South Sudan government and these groups who united their ranks during the negotiations and called themselves as 'South Sudan Opposition Movements' Alliance (SSOMA). Though Dr. Ismael Wais insisted that the Rome process remained 'under the IGAD rules of engagement,' the SSOMA group disavowed that proposal. They stated that they rejected the IGAD mediated R-ARCSS from the beginning and therefore couldn't be bound by IGAD's rules of engagement (Sudan Tribune, April 28, 2020).

6.7. The Revitalized Transitional Government of National Unity (R-TGoNU III)

After the signature of the R-ARCSS on September 12, 2018, a six-month pre-transitional period began. A joint National Pre-Transitional Committee (NPTC) composed of the government and opposition groups was appointed under Hon. Tut Gatluak Manimee. Their work mainly focused on the security arrangement which was to ensure that all forces (government and armed opposition) were to be trained and deployed before the formation of the Revitalized Transitional Government of National Unity (R-TGoNU) which is here denoted as TGoNU III.

The process began in a slow motion. The funds required to integrate all the forces were not forth coming. The Government of South Sudan had difficulty with cash flow due to economic crisis in the country. On the other hand, the international community took a wait-and-see posture without contributing any funds to the process. They felt that the parties were not going to implement the agreement in good faith and therefore did not want to commit their resources to it. For this reason, very small progress was made during the pre-transitional period.

Since the return of SPLM/A-IO leader Dr. Riek Machar to Juba was linked to the integration of forces, especially the Presidential Guards, it became clear that he would not come unless such prerequisite was fulfilled. As a consequence, an extension to the transitional period for six months was requested. After the acceptance of the request, the new deadline for formation of R-TGoNU fell on November 12, 2019. Even this new deadline was also extended as not much progress was made on the implementation of the pre-transitional issues. The new deadline for formation of R-TGoNU after the extension for the second time fell on February 22, 2020.

The issue of 32 states was still a lingering problem between the parties to the agreement. The point that the opposition made against the 32 states was that the 2015 ARCSS was signed on the basis of 10 states. The government pointed to the desire of the people of South Sudan to keep their states and their demand for even more.

The R-ARCSS provided a mechanism to address the issue of states and their boundaries. As a result, a boundary committee was established which was comprised of South Sudanese in government, opposition groups, IGAD, AU and representatives of non-African governments. The committee gauged the opinion of South Sudanese in their states and diaspora about whether or not 32 states should be kept. They found that South Sudanese inside and outside South Sudan wanted an increase to 49 states.

The other way for the committee to address this issue was for South Sudanese members of the committee to vote among themselves to decide the fate of the 32 states. Even though all the foreign representatives of the committee decided to vote in favour of the opposition interest contrary to the given rules and procedures, they failed to get the majority vote required to return the country to ten states. The AU and IGAD could not make a decision when the report of the committee was presented to them because the people of South Sudan wanted to keep their states and want to add even more.

In February, President Salva Kiir and the negotiating team of the Government of South Sudan went to Addis-Ababa to attend the meeting of the IGAD heads of State and Government on the implementation of R-ARCSS. There was too much pressure on the President to resolve the issue of the number of states as he was the only one left to rescue the country.

When the President returned to Juba from IGAD Summit in Addis-Ababa, he was welcomed in Juba international airport by huge number of citizens representing their states. He gave a very short speech at the airport stating that there was a lot of pressure from foreign powers to return the country to ten states. On February 4, 2020, people from the 32 states went to Freedom Hall to present their views and petition the President on the issue of states.

I was asked to be the Master of Ceremonies (MC) by the President on this occasion. We organized the meeting in such a way that people spoke first, followed by the President and thereafter the negotiating team members to provide context for the peace agreement. All the community leaders who spoke said that they wanted to keep their states and were demanding more.

It was time for the President to respond to them. He agreed with them that they should keep their states. However, he repeated what he said at the airport that the international pressure to reduce the number of states was heavy and that there was need to bring peace to the country. He presented a number of proposals which included: a reduction of the number of existing states by eliminating those states with land disputes; or return the country to ten states; or create some administrative areas, etc. He did not specify which course of action he was going to take.

After he finished his speech, he was expected to listen to the Chiefs that were due to speak. Instead, he suddenly got up and left the hall. In few seconds, First Vice President Taban Deng Gai also followed him. After a while, Vice President Dr. James Wani Igga also left. Being the MC for the occasion, I was left bewildered, standing in front of the people. Immediately, we asked Hon. Daniel Awet Akot, member of the SPLM Political Bureau, to chair the meeting. He obliged to our request. The negotiation team was seated in front of the people ready to speak. After their speeches, the people continued to talk demanding for more states, especially the communities of Raja and Anyuak.

After some hours, certain people became anxious as to why the leadership of the country left them without saying anything. Some of them started to come up to me asking whether the President and the Vice Presidents were going to return to the meeting. I said that they would send someone to talk to them later. I was not authorized by anyone to say this, but I did not want to indicate that none of us in front of them knew what was going on as that could have raised suspicion.

After almost two hours, Vice President Dr. James Wani came back to the meeting. I breathed a sigh of relief. I knew he came with a message from the President. He told the meeting the Presidency had just held a meeting and made a very important decision regarding the number of states which would be announced the next day.

The Freedom Hall experienced dead silence. It was the first time in TGoNU (II) that a decision was ever made and attributed to the Presidency. People did not know what to make of this information, but they continued to speak after Vice President Dr. James Wani left again. We collected their views and formulated the petition to be submitted to the President the next day. We did not know that this petition would never see the light of day.

In the morning of the 5th of February 2020, the Presidency announced that the country was returned to ten states and established three Administrative Areas (Ruwang and Greater Pibor Administrative areas as well as Abyei Special Administrative Area). All the people of South Sudan were shocked, but for the sake of peace, the Presidency was assured of the support of the SPLM, while the people of South Sudan stood firmly in support of their 32 states. On February 15, 2020, President Salva Kiir dissolved the 32 states by decree.

On February 21, 2020, the President also dissolved the Transitional Government of National Unity (TGoNU II) to give way for formation of the Revitalized Transitional Government of National Unity (R-TGoNU III). Despite the fact that the integration of forces was not completed, Dr. Machar decided to return to Juba to facilitate the formation of R-TGoNU. His security was entrusted to President Kiir by guarantors of the agreement. On February 22, 2020, Dr. Riek Machar was appointed as First Vice President of the Republic of South Sudan along with Dr. James Wani Igga, Taban Deng Gai, and Rebecca Nyandeng de' Mabior as Vice Presidents for designated clusters in the government. They took oath of office on the same day.

The South Sudan Opposition Alliance (SSOA) did not agree on one candidate to be appointed as Vice President. For that reason, they submitted six names from their leadership and authorized the President to pick whoever he wished from the submitted list to be Vice President. In the presence of H.E. Abdel Fatah Al Burhan, President of the Transitional Sovereign Council of the Sudan, who became Chair of IGAD after the ouster of President El Beshir, Hussein Abdelbagi Ayii Akol was appointed as Vice President on February 23, 2020 by President Kiir.

The 35-member National Cabinet was appointed on March 12, 2020 after a prolonged discussion on allocation of the ministerial portfolios between the government and the opposition parties. The portfolios were apportioned based on the formula provided for in the R-ARCSS.

In line with the agreement, the President dissolved the National Pre-Transitional Committee and replaced it with the National Transitional Committee (NTC) on March 27, 2020 headed by Tut Gatluak Manimee with the membership of the opposition parties to continue with the implementation of the remaining tasks of the defunct Pre-Transitional Committee.

In the same month, the corona virus (Covid-19) pandemic hit the country. The President appointed a high-level taskforce on March 12, 2020 to combat Covid-19. The taskforce was headed by First Vice President Dr. Riek Machar. However, on May 15, 2020, the President dissolved the taskforce and appointed a new one headed by Hussein Abdelbagi Ayii, the Vice President responsible for services cluster in the government. On 20 May, First Vice President Dr. Riek Machar, Minister of Defense Angelina Teny, Michael Makuei Lueth, Minister of information and other National Ministers tested positive for Covid-19. Later, Vice President Hussein Abdelbagi also tested positive for Covid-19.

According to the reports of the taskforce on combating Covid-19 and the WHO, South Sudan registered nearly 17, 051 cases, out of which 16, 913 recovered and 138 died by March 12, 2022 (WHO, March 12, 2022). This forced the Government of South Sudan to lockdown the country initially for one month from 3rd February to 3rd March 2021 then from the 3rd March to the 3rd of April 2021. The government continued to issue intermittent lockdowns in early 2022. The occurrence of the pandemic contributed to the slow implementation of the peace agreement as many cantonment sites were abandoned by the soldiers for fear of the spread of this disease in congested locations.

After the formation of the national government, the parties to the agreement divided the state gubernatorial portfolios according to the formula provided for in the agreement. What caused the delay in this process was deciding on which states would go to which parties as each of them had a strategic interest in certain states. Even after the states were divided, the nominee for the governorship of Upper Nile state became a spikey matter.

SPLM-IO nominee General Johnson Olony was rejected by

the Dinka Padang Community in Upper Nile for fear that he would use state government resources to fight them and take the disputed land between the two communities by force. The President also rejected the nomination of Gen. Johnson Olony for fear that a fight in Upper Nile would most likely cause the collapse of R-ARCSS in the country. The issue became a 'Mexican standoff' between the President and his First Deputy with no resolution in sight.

Dr. Machar was advised by many leaders that if this became the situation, he should appoint Gen. Olony as a National Minister and take someone from other communities of Upper Nile to be governor there. Even after nine governors and three chief administrators were appointed on June 29, 2020, Upper Nile remained without a governor for seven months. It was only on January 29, 2021 that Dr. Machar finally decided to replace General Johnson Olony with General Budhok Ayang Anei Kur as Governor of Upper Nile state. He was appointed by the President on the same day as governor.

The allocation of portfolios in the state government structures including the counties took longer than expected. Each time progress was made, some principals to the agreement would reject the proposal of the committee. Two years of the transitional period had already elapsed and only one year remained. There is clearly no way the remaining issues of the agreement would be resolved in one year prior to elections taking place. It would not surprise anyone if R-TGoNU will request an extension of the transitional period.

CHAPTER SEVEN

―――――――

Way Forward: Suggested priorities for implementation by the Government of South Sudan

THE PURPOSE FOR WHICH we liberated ourselves from domination was to be free and build a united democratic and prosperous country for ourselves (SPLM Manifesto, 2016). We did not seek freedom for its own sake, but to use it as a catalyst to advance our country and bring ourselves to be counted among the best nations of this earth.

The fact that we lost sight of our path and ventured into the unfortunate tragedy of destruction and war should not be an excuse to continue in that direction. All countries in their infancy have adventured into human development trajectory which is never linear. There are times when they lose sight of their goal, but then they find their way and continue in their journey. The experiences of the post-war United States and the reconstruction of the European countries in the aftermath of World War II should be lessons to teach us that losing one's path does not signal resignation, but the beginning of developing great nations. Former South African President, comrade Nelson Mandela, is known for saying that, 'The greatest glory in the living lies not in never falling, but in rising every time we fall.' He was talking about the power to persist in life and get up every day to fight over gain.

As a people, we have come too far to stop now. We fought for nearly a century for our freedom. We cannot look back, but learn from the past and move forward. I always say that the greatest strength of the people of South Sudan during the liberation struggle was always found at their weakest point. This means that when we realize our divisions cannot serve us, we always unite our ranks and face challenges with herculean effort. And we have always won when we turned away from perdition. This was demonstrated when disunity engulfed us in 1983 and 1991 and the enemy thought that the case of southern Sudan was over. We said, 'no' as this was only the beginning of the liberation struggle. As a result, we united our ranks in 1987 and almost liberated the entire territory of southern Sudan. When the same tragedy of disunity returned in 1991, we also came back together in 2002 and forced the Sudanese Government to sign the Comprehensive Peace Agreement which brought about our independence through the referendum. I am persuaded that we will also overcome the predicaments of 2013 and 2016 and move forward with our development agenda.

As we contemplate on the way forward for our country given the experience of the last fifteen years, it is important for our government to focus on the most important priorities which we could not live without. The list is not exhaustive, nor does it prevent any other agenda items to be included. However, we have learned in the last fifteen years that when we take everything as a national priority, we lose focus and end up without making any tangible developmental impact in our country. This is because we have very limited resources which cannot cover or pay for every development project simultaneously. Hence, the need to focus on the development of high impact physical infrastructure, mechanized agriculture, security reform and social priorities. These priorities are presented under each heading below for immediate and short-term action by the government.

7.1. Food Security Through Investment on Mechanized Agriculture

They say that a hungry man is an angry man. This is because no one listens when the stomach is empty. In other words, where poverty prevails, total peace and stability can not be expected. Food security in any society is the real security for all. Even if arms could be collected from the civil population and destroyed, security will remain untenable if the population continues to live in dire poverty. South Sudan is a potentially rich country. As South Sudan National Dialogue Econmic Cluster stated: (ND economy, 2020, p. 2):

South Sudan is endowed with all kinds of natural resources such as water, fish, wildlife, cattle, arable land, solar, wind, hydroelectric potential, etc. It also has forest, forest products such as Gum-Arabic, honey, lulu and all kinds of mineral resources such as oil, gas, diamonds, limestone, irone ore, copper, chromium ore, zinc, tungsten, mica, silver, etc.

Oil and minerals are, but a few of the natural resources whose proceeds can be used to fuel the expansion of the agricultural sector which is the mainstay of the economy. Therefore, one of the top priorities of any government in South Sudan must be to promote mechanized agricultural development using public-private partnerships and provide seeds for individuals and cooperative farmers.

South Sudan's Government thus far has not adequately invested in the agricultural sector. The Presidential project which distributed tractors to the states for agricultural development in 2016 was a welcomed initiative. However, due to insecurity in the country, those implements were not put to use in Greater Upper Nile and Greater Equatoria regions. Unless South Sudan loosens the grip of poverty on its population, insecurity cannot be effectively curtailed.

7.2. Physical Infrastructure Development

For the last 15 years, South Sudan has not succeeded in the area of physical infrastructure development. In fact, underdevelopment has been an indelible mark on the region since time immemorial. When the Government of southern Sudan was formed in 2005, every development project was considered a national priority. Education, health, roads, electricity, agriculture, clean drinking water, dams, bridges, etc., were all critical components of the national development agenda. This multiplicity of priorities created confusion among policy makers as to which project would take the first slot. The policy makers were not able to discern the most important development programs from the menu of priorities.

A good start could have been on road construction, mechanized agriculture and electricity generation which are believed to be *sine qua non* to stimulate economic growth and development. Roads are the veins for transportation of agricultural products and goods. Without a network of roads which connect principal towns with the agricultural centers where production happens, real development would remain elusive.

The same case could be made for electricity generation. South Sudan is one of the few countries in the world which still depends on generators for energy production. Not only is this environmentally degrading, but also expensive. In the absence of hydroelectric power generation or some sort of single source power production for the country, industrial, agricultural, and other significant investments would not be possible. If the Government of South Sudan is to promote development, it must prioritize mechanized agriculture, road construction and production of electricity.

7.3. Security Sector Reform

Security problems in Africa are caused by diversity suppression, lack of equitable distribution of national wealth, poor governance and proliferation of poverty. Those who perceive that they are discriminated against or dominated, usually fight against the existing government for, "access to power, resources and services" (Deng, 2018, p.16).

In the case of South Sudan, differences amongst the leaders of the SPLM/A have caused security problems in the country. This was manifested in 1983 and 1991 when the SPLM split due to ideological differences surrounding the objectives of the movement and the leadership question. These political contradictions in the movement resulted in conflict which was characterized as setting Dinka against Nuer. That predicament almost crippled the national liberation struggle against the Sudanese government in the 1980s and 1990s (Both, 2003).

The SPLM repeated this tragedy for the third time immediately after independence in 2013. The same leadership rivalry within the party was also the main cause. This again pitted the Dinka against the Nuer as the two protagonists. This is because there is a tendency by the leaders of the party to manipulate internal differences within the SPLM and turn them into ethnic differences.

When policy differences of the party are turned into ethnic differences, they are difficult to resolve as the party itself ceases to exist. Even though party officials, institutions and other mechanisms may exist, discussions and deliberations on national issues tend to be marred with ethnic overtures rather than focusing on substantive issues which could benefit the people and the country.

In line with this backdrop, South Sudan suffered from insecurity. When the SPLM/A split in 1983 and 1991, many of the leaders of the SPLM splinter groups formed their own military and ideological groups which were armed and used by the Sudanese Government in an attempt to destroy the SPLM/A mainstream. After the conclusion of the 2005 Comprehensive Peace Agreement, the utility of these groups became increasingly irrelevant to the Sudanese Government. Hence, they started to negotiate with the then Government of southern Sudan which resulted in their integration beginning in 2006 into the SPLA.

It was reported that the number of integrated militia forces surpassed those in the mother SPLA. The majority of these militias were not trained soldiers, but self-promoted individuals with high military ranks. Some of them joined the militia groups during the integration process into the SPLA as it was viewed as an employment opportunity for unskilled workers. The political leaders of militia groups were given positions in government and the SPLA at the expense of the loyal and committed members of the SPLM/A. As Deng (2018, p.38) articulated:

> *President Salva Kiir Mayardit made the unity of the country his top priority by absorbing armed militias into the SPLA. This was highly applauded, but it proved paradoxically a source of ongoing disunity and chronic violence as ambitious commanders saw rebellion as a rewarding adventure.*

In this sense, 'militarism' became a lucrative business in South Sudan. If one wanted to be a General or Minister in the government, all that one needed to do was to rebel with a few henchmen and wreak havoc. Thereafter, a decree would be issued by the President to declare a general amnesty for all those who took up arms against the government. Then the militia leaders would take advantage of this and subsequently would be made Generals or Ministers and the cycle would continue for those who may feel discontent in the future.

This 'big tent approach' (Johnson, 2016) became a major source of insecurity as the SPLA became an army of divided loyalties. The various militia groups that were integrated into it were still loyal to their former commanders who now became Generals in all the organized forces or Ministers in the Government of South Sudan.

The orders of the SPLA command were to be checked first with their former leaders before they could enforce them. This indiscipline manifested itself in 2013, when the then SPLA Chief of General Staff, Gen. James Hoth Mai issued orders for restraint and calm during the crisis, but the former Nuer and Dinka militias could not obey orders. They were clearly commanded by their former leaders, and this was what escalated the 2013 crisis in Juba.

In order to alleviate insecurity in the country, the three regional and national conferences of South Sudan National Dialogue unanimously called for the professionalization of the SPLA and other organized forces in the country (ND Book six, 2020; Resolution of the ND national conference, 2020). This exercise would involve purging the unfit; retiring high ranking officers; and training the retained qualified cadres. Some strict criteria to join the army and other organized forces needed to be developed so that only the best could enter the army and other organized forces to serve the country.

There should also be programs that would address the needs

of the purged cadres so that they do not end up in arms again. This requires resources to be dedicated from the government and the international community so that the issue of insecurity in South Sudan can be amicably addressed.

The second exercise would be to disarm the civil population which was endeavored in the past without substantive success. This issue was agreed by consensus during the three regional and national conferences of South Sudan National Dialogue (ND Book six 2020; Resolution of the ND national conference, 2020). There was a mixed reaction to the disarmement exercise when it was attempted from March to August 2012. Certain leaders within the South Sudan Government were reluctant to accept disarmament because they could not guarantee protection for their ethnic communities. In some states, where disarmament almost became successful, certain Generals within the organized forces and Ministers in the Government of South Sudan re-armed their communities. As disarmament was not conducted simultaneously across the country, certain communities that were not disarmed quickly took advantage by killing people; abducting women and children; and stealing cattle.

The international community was ambivalent towards a civilian disarmament exercise conducted in South Sudan in 2012. Initially, they supported the move and were ready to provide funds as incentives for those who voluntarily agreed to disarm. However, they did not agree with the SPLA's forceful disarmament which was instituted after it was clear that the local chiefs could not persuade the youth to disarm. This operation resulted in violence and displacement of local people. This was particularly acute in Jonglei state where army and civilians engaged in fighting which resulted in untold suffering.

Due to inter-clan fighting, a small-scale disarmament exercise was also carried out in 2020 by South Sudan People's Defense Forces (SSPDF), formerly known as SPLA, in Warrap and Lakes States, with minimal success. Next time around, civilian disarmament needs to be well conceptualized. There are lessons to learn from what was done in other parts of the world. The UNDDR program could be a great asset to provide expertise on this exercise.

Moreover, the Government of South Sudan for all practical purposes would not be able to carry out civilian disarmament by itself. It may request technical assistance on disarmament from the region and international community by providing resources and capability to collect guns from the civilian population simultaneously so that no community would be left vulnerable to attacks by another which is not yet disarmed.

Furthermore, the participation of regional and international actors in the disarmament exercise may build confidence in the population to give up their arms. Those who voluntarily bring their guns to the authorities should be given incentives as a motivation.

The people of South Sudan in the three regional and national conferences of the National Dialogue suggested that the Government of South Sudan needs to replace AK-47 weapon system for another one so that once the weapons in the hands of the civil population are collected, ammunitions would not be easily found in the country. In this way, insecurity would be significantly reduced.

7.4. Reinforcement of Customary Democratic Values

Democracy is not a foreign concept to the people of South Sudan and Africans in general. What could be foreign to many may be the Greek word '*democracy*' and not the practice of it. In many cultures of South Sudan, men and women come under a tree and discuss their issues with everyone's participation valued and recognized. This discussion could go on for days if no consensus was reached or if the majority of the people were not persuaded on an issue. This is participatory democracy in action.

When this practice involves elections, people come together in one location and the candidates would stand in rows and those who support a particular candidate would line up behind the person of their choice. Voters were head counted and losers would know their fate before results could be announced because they could see the number of their supporters lined up behind them. Once this was done, those who did not win accept defeat and life returns to normal for everyone in the village. Some of the elements of our traditional democracy also include modern approaches such as openness, good governance, freedom of speech, assembly, political pluralism, and the rule of law.

An important element in our cultures is the principle of openness. The people of South Sudan are vocal. They speak their minds on issues which affect them. Therefore, our political system must avail space for such expression to take place and be protected by the constitution. This freedom includes the freedom of the press to ensure that all branches of government and private sector are held to account by the public. Freedom of the press must be guaranteed and safeguarded by law.

Political pluralism is another aspect of a democratic society. In a country like South Sudan where there are various issues which affect people disproportionately or otherwise, multiple political opinions exist on how to address them, and that situation calls for an allowance of a multiparty system to take hold in the country. South Sudan must permit this kind of expression so that people are able to choose from a menu of parties that prescribe to a variety of manifestos and ideologies.

It should be entirely up to an individual to choose a party of his/her choice. The disadvantage of political pluralism in Africa as stated elsewhere in this book is that political parties are established along ethnic lines rather than on ideology or substantive issues. This is because the levels of education and understanding of issues are still at a rudimentary stage.

7.5. Appreciation for Ethnic Diversity

African leadership since the time of liberation struggle viewed ethnic groups or tribes as divisive elements which must be contained (Deng, 2018). This was because during these national liberation struggles, the African people were united by the need to free themselves from colonial exploitation. Fighting for freedom against a common enemy became such an overriding issue that it masked the existence of ethnic, cultural and other differences that existed among groups of people in a given African country.

However, the issue of ethnicity and tribes could not be wished away by African leadership. It was something which existed and needed to be recognized. Recognition of diversity means that all ethnic groups and people with special needs must have equal access to power structures and national resources in all sectors of society, in order to make unity of a country strong and attractive. Diversity and national unity are not antithetical concepts as African leadership thought. It is tribalism which threatens national unity and stability, not the tribes per se. Tribalism therefore is a manipulative method used by political leaders to mobilize their ethnic groups against others in order to gain their political objectives in a given country.

In the case of South Sudan, it is recognized that there are 64 or more ethnic groups in the country. This should serve as a blessing because the country would utilize different skills, knowledge, expertise, and experience of its diverse population for development.

In fighting tribalism, our political system, as a matter of policy, must mainstream ethnic representation, gender equality and equitable access to development resources across various states in the country. South Sudan must also reduce tribalism through the utilization of political party system, civic education, policy, and the law. Once diversity is recognized and mainstreamed, the perception of marginalization, ethnic domination and imbalanced development would fade away from the minds of various groups in the country.

The form and type of governance model which should guide the people of South Sudan must be based on their own experience as a people given their history of being recognized by various anthropologists as "segmentary, acephalous, decentralized, self-governing and fiercely antagonistic to centralized authoritarian rule" (Deng, 2018, p.17). Even though in the National Dialogue conference conducted from November

3-17, 2020, the people of South Sudan across the three regions of Upper Nile, Equatoria and Bahr El Ghazal endorsed federalism as a preferred system of governance for South Sudan, the details of such are left out for technical experts to expound. It may be possible in the final analysis that this will be a hybrid of South Sudanese experience with western elements of federalism married to it.

7.6. Inter-Communal Dialogue and Reconciliation

South Sudan is made up of about 64 known ethnic groups speaking a variety of national languages. Before the liberation struggle, these groups used to live peacefully with each other. In those days, individuals used to traverse long distances on foot without any fear. People were friendly and respectful of human life and property as guided by their local cultures. Even cattle would be driven from Bahr El Ghazal to Upper Nile and from Upper Nile to Equatoria without problems.

However, during the national liberation struggle against the Sudanese Government, those cultural values were almost eroded as atrocities were committed against different individuals and communities. In accordance with the rules of war in the majority of cultures in South Sudan, women, elders, and children were off limits. Rape was a taboo act and any perpetrator of such was immediately punished or banished from the community. No warrior could be praised for attacking the most vulnerable in society as this was an action by a coward.

Nonetheless, the good old days of social tranquility and harmony were gone. Social relations between and among communities and tribes were strained as cultural values slowly emaciated. Community elders who used to be the vanguards of community customs, values and traditions were no longer doing their duty as youth with guns wreaked havoc in their communities. More often than not, elders have become military commanders who no longer viewed themselves as protectors of community values, norms and traditions. In some circumstances, they encouraged the youth to commit atrocities instead of giving them advice to restrain from subversive activities. Inter-communal trust and tranquility which used to exist was replaced by fear and suspicion of each other and that continued to be the source of insecurity in the country.

In order to address this predicament, the people of South Sudan in the National Dialogue's regional and national conferences (Book six, 2020; Resolutions of ND national conference, 2020) endorsed the need to engage in continuous dialogue and discussion among various communities in order to address their fears and suspicion to restore positive relations. The government and the international community need to be at the center of this through funding and facilitation of the inter-communal dialogue. Once trust is restored and social infrastructure is repaired, peace and stability would return to the country.

7.7 Accountability and Transparency

The concept of good governance is rooted in the cultures of traditional South Sudan. It is morally wrong for someone to take something that does not belong to him/her. The practice of thievery is extremely disdained. In fact, if one is known as a thief, the stigma is attached not only to that person, but also to their entire family. The scorn is so much that no one wants to marry in or from that family because of such negative repute.

In the context of modern governance system, public properties belong to all people. Therefore, taking something from public coffers is the same as stealing in the community and the doer of such act must be ostracized by the people and the law. If the precepts of good governance in our traditional society are married to the safeguards of modern good governance system, there will be enough resources to develop our country and services would be available to all the communities.

At the moment, there is rarely any book or article written on South Sudan recently that would not touch on the lack of good governance and accountability. South Sudan's government officials have been accused of graft and carelessness in the way they have managed public resources.

I had a disconcerting conversation with a friend from a western country who contended that the reason why South Sudanese were fond of government positions is because they wanted to enrich themselves at the expense of the public. I felt that his comments were directed to certain individuals he had in mind in the government, especially after the release of various reports by The Sentry (2016) accusing predominantly Dinka and Nuer leaders in the Government of South Sudan of corruption. While the reports of this agency were dismissed as biased towards the two ethnic groups by their interlocutors who have South Sudanese opposition connections, the fact remains that corruption has become pervasive in the country.

However, this friend put me on an unnecessary defense. My response was that not all the officials of the Government of South Sudan mismanaged public resources. There were government officials who did not acquire wealth illegally at the

expense of the public. In fact, there were people who left opportunities elsewhere and came to South Sudan to suffer with
their people.

After giving some practical examples of such officials who
did well in the public service sector, he retracted some of his
harsh views. However, the point remains that the perception
of corruption in South Sudan is far reaching. In some cases,
the perpetrators were brought to justice while others remained
mere allegations which were not presented in a court of law.

All the same, public resources entrusted to officials should
be used for programs which benefit the public. The problem
which manifested itself in South Sudan was that budgetary
guidelines were not followed by ministries at various levels of
government. Instititions of government spent money on items
which were not budgeted. Some of them overspend while
others underspend dependent on the relationship between the
head of a particular institution with the existing Minister of
Finance at various levels of government in the country. No
questions were asked to explain this phenomenon due to weak
oversight of the Legislative Assemblies at all levels of government. Fiscal guidelines and spending policies need to be strictly
followed if the country is to get out of financial malpractice.

Another aspect which infringes on poor management of
public resources is the culture of some South Sudanese ethnic
groups. Some cultures in South Sudan believe that if a Minister
is from their community, that position belongs to them, and
many would come and live in the house of the Minister. They
would also expect their school fees and health bills to be paid by
that Minister. Furthermore, the same official is also expected to
contribute significantly to their marriage dowries. It is difficult

for the salary of a Minister to defray all these expenses without infringing on public resources. As Deng (2018, p.39) observed:

> *When a senior government official or military officer is seen by his impoverished people as a potential benefactor in providing for their essential needs, and he has access to public resources, temptations can become difficult to resist. The line between wrong and right becomes quite thin. Not very many people have the moral fortitude to resist crossing that thin line.*

Financial assistance for the vulnerable citizens in our country is another issue to ponder. South Sudan is a country with large numbers of vulnerable groups such as widows, orphans, street children, war disabled and wounded veterans from the liberation struggle for independence. However, there is no social welfare system in which the government can take care of the most vulnerable in society as a matter of policy due to the financial status of the young nation. For that reason, the Ministries of Social Welfare at all levels of government do not have any funds to assist these groups. Therefore, social support remains predominantly a service provided by family members, relatives and friends.

Nevertheless, this does not mean that vulnerable people do not get financial assistance from government institutions. In fact, they are assisted on individual basis by various institutions of government even though such items are not budgeted. These are the people who (or whose parents) liberated this country and through this process, got widowed, orphaned or disabled to the point where they could not provide for themselves. As such, government officials, who are most of the times former colleagues or friends of their deceased parents are morally obliged to assist them even though it is against financial regulations. This financial malpractice, necessitated by compassion and kindness towards those who gave so much for this country, has gotten so many government officials in trouble by the way they handled public resources. While it is morally good for officials to provide financial assistance to the vulnerable, the practice is against the law.

Put in another way, this type of unoffical financial assistance by government officials, could explain why massive corruption in South Sudan is reported, and yet little is done about it. Therefore, when corruption is discussed in the context of South Sudan, some of these contextual complexities need to be at the heart of the analysis.

7.8. Conclusion

This book has tried to address four important issues which are central to the understanding of conflict in South Sudan. These include: (a) the imperative of the constitutional change of government, (b) the need to build an international relationship that is based on mutual respect and understanding using the principles of constructive engagement, (c) the depiction of the ethnic communities in South Sudan as victims, and (d) the scapegoating of the SPLM as a villain in this war.

The people of South Sudan fought against repressive regimes for nearly half a century in order to gain freedom and establish their own democratic state based on the rule of law. The envisioned state was to be governed by the National Constitution which safeguards social, cultural and political liberties which can only be attained if the country is in the state of peace and stability. Ensuring that political stability means that the political protagonists must adhere to the principles of the rule of law as enshrined in the National Constitution.

No matter how dysfunctional the Government of South Sudan has become, it never makes it legal for any group to change it by means of arms. If overzealous politicians are allowed to circumvent constitutional processes to change the government, there will never be political stability in South Sudan. That was the reason why the majority of the leaders of the Nuer community in the SPLM did not agree with the 2013 group to force the government of President Salva Kiir out of office by unconstitutional means. He was the elected President and only another election can remove him from office. Therefore, the imperative of constitutional change of government must be upheld by all groups in the country.

Second, since the start of the conflict in South Sudan, there has been regional and international action to end the war in the country. Such interventions were in the form of peace negotiations, SPLM reunification process, security, and humanitarian assistance. Such actions could have been impactful if the region and the international community endeavored to win the co-operation of the government and the people of South Sudan. Forced intervention or resistance to intervention can only end in failure as the capacity of all sides to respond to the crisis in a meaningful way will be drained.

The region and the international community have been cynical on the will of the leaders of South Sudan to resolve the conflict and bring peace to the country. For that reason, they decide not to support peace implementation processes by declining to avail resources to that effect. They tend to say publicly that they stand with the people of South Sudan. This by implication means that they do not want to cooperate with the Government of South Sudan to bring peace to the country.

Similarly, the leaders of the Government of South Sudan are also apprehensive about the intentions of the region and the international community to intervene in the internal affairs of the country. For any intervention to be successful and for it to be in the best interest of the people of South Sudan, cooperation with the government is pivotal since the mutual aim of all parties is to bring peace to the country.

Thirdly, the conflict which has been raging in our country for the last seven years is described as senseless because there is nothing in it for the people of South Sudan. However, it makes sense for the leaders who are fighting to acquire powerful political positions in the government. In this regard, the people of South Sudan become victims of this opportunistic ambition disguised as national interest which is pursued by pitting ethnic groups against each other. This political opportunism was laid bare by the signature of the 2015 ARCSS and its revitalized successor, the R-ARCSS, which are largely about power sharing among the leaders of this country. The delay to implement other chapters of the agreement, which have nothing to do with personal benefits of the leaders, was not inadvertent. Therefore, the war for them cannot be described as senseless.

The worst that could happen to the people of South Sudan would be if they didn't learn anything from this conflict experience as they gaze into the future. They are set against each other for war that has nothing to do with them. This should make them vigilant and learn to address conflict through reconciliation and dialogue even if their political leaders opt for military confrontation. There has never been an inherent conflict between and among ethnic groups in South Sudan. This phenomenon emerged during the national liberation struggle when some ethnic communities identified with particular personalities from their ethnic groups in the SPLM/A. For instance, a larges scale communal conflict between Nuer and Dinka never existed until Dr. Riek Machar clashed with the then Chairman of the SPLM Dr. John Garang in 1991 and with the current Chairman of the SPLM President Salva Kiir Mayardit in 2013. Both conflicts were caused by Dr. Riek Machar's proclivity to ascend to political power by means of arms in the SPLM/A.

Finally, another victim in this conflict is the ruling party in South Sudan, the SPLM itself. There is a great deal of misconception in this country that the SPLM has failed the people of South Sudan. However, this book has pointed to the abandoned vision of the SPLM as the only way forward, with a promise to build a united, democratic and prosperous South Sudan with clear mission to accomplish it. The fact that this vision has not been implemented is not a failure of the SPLM, but its cadres in the leadership who decided not to utilize the institutions of the party to drive development and provide services to the people in the country. The blame must rest on those responsible and the SPLM as an institution must be vindicated. There are also those who have developed a negative attitude towards the SPLM because its leaders hail from certain communities whom they perceive as benefiting from state resources. This assumption is also objectively wrong. The SPLM is not a tribal political party and the communities from which its leaders hail are as destitute as any other communities in South Sudan in terms of lack of development and service provision.

SPLM cadres in leadership should be persuaded to implement the basic objectives for which the country was liberated. Some of these objectives are partially captured in this book. Re-discovering those objectives will result in the establishment of a united, democratic and prosperous country for which we fought to build.

REFERENCES

African Union Commission of Inquiry on South Sudan
(2014). Final Report of the African Union Commission
of Inquiry on South Sudan. African Union Headquarters,
Addis-Ababa, Ethiopia.

African Union-Led Regional Taskforce (2011). Regional
Cooperation Initiative for Elimination of LRA.
Africa Union Headquarters, Addis-Ababa, Ethiopia.
Retrieved on 27 December 2020 from www.peaceau.
org>page>100>au-led-rci-lra-1.

Aleu, Ayieny Aleu (2008). Letter to Cde. Pa'gan Amum
Okiech, SPLM Secretary General.26 January 2008.
Khartoum, Sudan.

Amnesty International (1995). Sudan: The tears of orphans:
No future without human rights. Retrieved on 9 March
2021 from https://www.amnesty.org/en/documents/
AFR54/002/1995/en/

Both, Peter Lam (2003). South Sudan: Forgotten Tragedy.

Author House, Bloomington, Indiana. United States of America.

Clapham, Christopher (2012). From liberation Movement to Government: Past legacies and the challenge of transition in Africa. The Brenthurst Foundation, Discussion Paper 8/12, Johannesburg, South Africa.

Deng, Francis Mading (2020). Visitations: Conversations with the ghost of the Chairman. Red Sea Press. Trenton, New Jersey, United States of America.

Deng, Francis Mading, et al. (ed.) (2020). Abyei between two Sudans. Red Sea Press. Trenton, New Jersey, United States of America.

Deng, Francis Mading (2018). Reflections on South Sudan National Dialogue. South Sudan National Dialogue Steering Committee. Juba, South Sudan.

Deng, Francis Mading (1982). Security problems: An African predicament. 13th Annual Hans Wolff Memorial Lecture on October 23, 1981. African Studies Program, Indiana University. Bloomington, Indiana, United States.

Deng, Lual Achuek (2020). The National Dialogue: Framework for sustainable peace, economic growth and poverty eradication in South Sudan. Africa World Books Pty Ltd. Osborne Park, Australia.

Deng, William Deng (2013). Letter of Advice to Dr. Riek Machar. 12 April 2013, Juba, South Sudan.

Edwards, Tim (2016). Bloody Nile: How South Sudan imploded just two years after independence. Bullseye Publication Corporation. New York, United States of America.

Friends of the SPLM/A (2013). Letter sent to President

Salva Kiir Mayardit warning him against the direction
the country was taking. 24 June 2013, Washington, DC.
United States.

Human Rights Watch (2016). South Sudan: New abuses of
human rights by both sides. Printed in the United States of
America.

Human Rights Watch (2014). South Sudan's new war: Abuses
by Government and Opposition forces. Printed in the
United States of America.

IGAD (2013). Communiqué of the 23rd Extraordinary Session
of the IGAD Assembly of Heads of State and Government
on the situation in South Sudan. State House, Nairobi,
Kenya.

Johnson, Hilde F. (2016). South Sudan: The untold story
from independence to the civil war. I.B Tauris Publishing
Company. London, United Kingdom.

Khalid, Mansour (ed.) (1987). John Garang speaks. London. KPI.

Kuol, Deng Alor (2020). A diplomat turned warrior. In F. M.
Deng, L.B.D. Kuol and D. J. Deng, (Eds.), *Abyei between
two Sudans* (pp.39-60). Red Sea Press. Trenton, New Jersey,
United States of America.

Kuol, Luka Biong Deng (2020). The Abyei Arbitration. In
F. M. Deng, L.B.D. Kuol and D. J. Deng, (Eds.), *Abyei
between two Sudans* (pp.189-208). Red Sea Press. Trenton,
New Jersey, United States of America.

Kuol, Arop Deng (2020). Frontline invisible diplomat. In
F. M. Deng, L.B. D. Kuol and D. J. Deng, (Eds.), *Abyei
between two Sudans* (pp. 101-135). Red Sea Press. Trenton,
New Jersey, United States of America.

Lok, Nhial Biel (2016). Survivor of Juba massacre: Survivors investigation by Human Rights Watch in South Sudan. Nhial Biel Lok.

Malwal, Bona (2017). Abyei of the Ngok Dinka: Not yet South Sudan. Bourchier, Malmesbury, England, United Kingdom.

Nyaba, Peter Adwok (Rev. ed.) (2017). South Sudan: The State we aspire to. Africa World Books Pty Ltd. Osborne Park, Australia.

Nyaba, Peter Adwok (2016). South Sudan: Crisis of infancy. Rafiki Trading and Investment Company Ltd. South Sudan.

Nyaba, Peter Adwok (1996). The politics of liberation in South Sudan: An insiders' view. Fountain Publishers. Kampala, Uganda.

Pendle, Naomi R. (2020). The 'Nuer of Dinka money' and the demands of the dead: Contesting the morale limits of monetized politics in South Sudan. *Conflict, security and development, 2020.* Vol. 20, 5, 587–605. https://doi.org/10.1 0801/14678802.2020.1820161

Pinaud, Celemence (2021). War and genocide in South Sudan. Ithaca. Cornell University Press.

South Sudan Bureau of Statistics (2008). South Sudan Population and Housing Census, 2008. National Bureau of Statistics Headquarters. Juba, South Sudan.

South Sudan Human Rights Commission (2015). Interim Report on South Sudan internal conflict from 15 December 2013 to 15 March 2014. SSHRC Headquarters, Juba, South Sudan.

South Sudan Ministry of Finance and Economic Planning (2016). South Sudan Development Plan for 2016-2018. Ministry of Finance and Economic Planning, Republic of

South Sudan, Juba.

South Sudan Ministry of Finance and Economic Planning (2011). South Sudan Development Plan for 2011-2013. Ministry of Finance and Economic Planning, Republic of South Sudan, Juba.

South Sudan National Dialogue (2020). Recommendations on completing the implementation of the CPA. Recommendations of the National Dialogue Conference to R-TGoNU. National Dialogue Steering Committee. Juba, Republic of South Sudan.

South Sudan National Dialogue (2020). Resolutions of the National Dialogue Conference conducted from 3-17 November 2020. National Dialogue Steering Committee. Juba, Republic of South Sudan.

South Sudan National Dialogue (2020). Building a shared vision for the new nation. South Sudan

National Dialogue Steering Committee. Juba, Republic of South Sudan.

South Sudan National Dialogue (2020). Transformation of the Economy of South Sudan. South Sudan National Dialogue Steering Committee. Juba, Republic of South Sudan.

South Sudan National Dialogue (2020). Book six: Recommendations of the three Regional Conferences of Bahr El Ghazal, Upper Nile and Equatoria. National Dialogue Steering Committee. Juba, Republic of South Sudan.

SPLM Economic Commission (2004). SPLM strategic framework for war to peace transition. New Site, Kapoeta County, southern Sudan.

SPLM Rumbek Meeting (2004). Confidential report on

the Rumbek joint meeting of the SPLM/A Leadership Council, General Military Command Council, Heads of Commissions, SPLM Secretariats, SPLM County Secretaries, Civil Society and Community Leaders from 29 November to 1 December 2004. Rumbek, Lakes, State, southern Sudan.

Sudan Tribune (2016). Heavy casualties reported on J1 clashes in Juba. https://sudantribune.com/spip.php?article59551. 9 July 2016 retrieved on 29 December 2020.

Sudan Tribune (2013). Senior SPLM colleagues give Kiir ultimatum over the party crisis. https://sudantribune.com/spip.php?iframe&page=imprimable&id_article=49087. 6 December 2013 retrieved on 27 December 2020.

Sudan Tribune (2013). African Union says Abyei unilateral referendum "illegal." https://sudantribune.com/spip.php?article48603. 28 October 2013 retrived on 28 December 2020

Sudan Tribune (2012). South Sudan Vice President confirms apology for Bor massacre. https://sudantribune.com/South-Sudan-VP-confirms-apology, 42124. 4April 2012 retrieved on 27 December 2020.

Teny, Riek Machar (1994). South Sudan: A history of political domination- A case for self-determination. Retrieved on 16 December 2020 from www.africa.upenn.edu.

The Sentry (2016). War crimes shouldn't pay: Stopping the looting and destruction in South Sudan. An investigative Report. The Sentry. United States of America. Retrieved on 20 December 2020 from https://thesentry.org/reports/warcrimesshouldntpay/

Thiong, Daniel Akech (2021). The politics of fear in South Sudan: Generating chaos, creating conflict. Zed Books,

London, United Kingdom.

United Nations Mission in South Sudan (2016). Conflict in South Sudan: A human rights report. UNMISS Human Rights Division, Republic of South Sudan, Juba.

United Nations Mission in South Sudan (2014). Conflict in South Sudan: A human rights report. UNMISS Human Rights Division, Republic of South Sudan, Juba.

WHO (2021). South Sudan Coronavirus (COVID-19) statistics. Total and daily confirmed cases and deaths. Retrieved on 2 April 2021 from www.covid-19.who. int>afro>country>ss.

Yoh, John Gai (2015). Playing Angels. Black rain, Nairobi, Kenya.

Young, John (2019). South Sudan's civil war: Violence, insurgency and failed peacemaking. Zed Books. London, United Kingdom.

INDEX

ABOUT THE AUTHOR

PETER LAM BOTH has been SPLM Interim Secretary General since September 2021. Prior to this, he held the portfolios of Acting Secretary for Administration and Finance in the SPLM (2019-2021); Secretary for Culture, Information and Communications (2017-2019); first Governor of (now defunct) Latjor state, (2015-2017) when South Sudan was divided into 28 states; Minister for Information, Communications and Broadcasting in Upper Nile state (2010-2012); SPLM National Deputy Secretary for External Affairs (2009-2010) and SPLM Representative to Canada (2006-2009).

Furthermore, he served as Chairperson of South Sudan Relief and Rehabilitation Commission (SSRRC), (2012-2013), responsible for 91 offices across the country, and also worked in the humanitarian and development sector, as an expert, with the UNHCR on intermittent missions in Ethiopia, India and Jordan spanning from 1996-2005.

Peter graduated with a Bachelor's (Honors) degree in Political Science and International Relations from Addis-Ababa University in 1996; and from the University of Calgary in Alberta, Canada with a Bachelor of Social Work (BSW) in 2002, and a Master of Social Work (MSW) in 2004. He authored South Sudan: Forgotten Tragedy (2003) and International Relations of Ethiopia (2004) as well as co-authored peer reviewed articles in the Journal of Social Work and Journal of Educational Action Research in 2008.

Peter has also taught at the University of Calgary, Mount Royal University and University of Lethbridge in Alberta, Canada.

www.ingramcontent.com/pod-product-compliance
Lightning Source LLC
Chambersburg PA
CBHW021855020426
42334CB00013B/337